GOD
HEARS YOUR
PETTY
PRAYERS

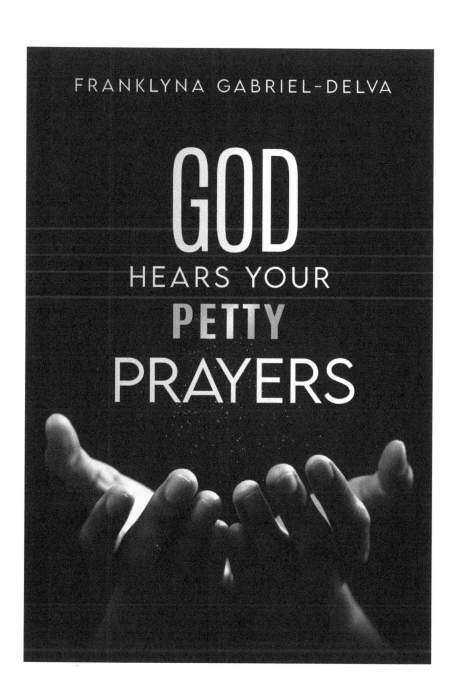

FRANKLYNA GABRIEL-DELVA

GOD
HEARS YOUR
PETTY
PRAYERS

XULON PRESS

Xulon Press
2301 Lucien Way #415
Maitland, FL 32751
407.339.4217
www.xulonpress.com

Printed in the United States of America

Paperback ISBN-13: 978-1-6628-4028-9
Ebook ISBN-13: 978-1-6628-4029-6

I once came across a quote that reads, "Pettiness is the tendency of people without large purposes."
- George F. Will
(https://www.azquotes.com/quote/1269289,
Accessed December 1, 2021)

That may be true in many cases, but in prayer, pettiness is the tendency of people aware of God's grand purpose.

Franklyna Gabriel-Delva

For Tony. My husband and PIPP (Partner in Petty Prayer)

Table of Contents

Prayer First

Heavenly Father,

I ask that Your presence be all over these pages. Touch every nook and cranny. My prayer is that no stone will be left unturned in my life or in the life of the reader. I pray that You take a personal step toward us as we take a giant leap toward You in faith for every single detail of our lives. Lord, may our petty prayers be heard, processed, and brought to fruition in our daily walks. May we depend on You for everything big and small. May Your light shine on us and through us so that our good works may glorify our Father in Heaven. Be with us in all that we do, in all that we say, and all that we need. Be with us when we don't even know what to ask for. Meet us in that secret place and carry us to victory.

Amen

Petty

Of little Importance; Trivial[1]

"A Lion does not turn around when a dog barks"~
African Proverb

I have a confession to make. I am petty. I confess that whenever I'm wronged, there's a little voice inside my head that whispers, "This person needs to feel the same pain they caused me, that's the only way they'll learn." Now, that little voice might be a little louder than we Christians would like to admit, but it's there and in full effect if left unchecked. We don't want it to be, but we're human, and our flesh, though crucified with Jesus, is still a problem for us until the day we get our glorified bodies. If we're being honest, some of us embrace that voice at full speed with no regrets and ask for forgiveness later.

Thankfully, I'm no longer a reckless teenager in age or maturity level and the Lord has brought me a long way. Now

---

[1] Lexico Dictionaries. (n.d.). Petty English definition and meaning. Lexico Dictionaries | English. Retrieved March 15, 2021, from https://www.lexico.com/en/definition/petty.

I can just say, "Bless his heart," knowing that I have to apologize to the Lord later for what I really wanted to say.

Without God, there is no way I can live in this frustrating world without blowing up. If I'm being honest, I love people, but I don't like them very much. This includes myself. Sure, there are people I like but not all the time. The way I see it, the Lord said to love our neighbors. He never said anything about "liking" people. Don't get me wrong, I love to help people, I love talking to people, I love being around those I love, and I care for the less fortunate. I do all the things Jesus told us to do in love but somewhere, I realized, I didn't like people. It was weird to me because I love being around them, I love talking, and I am someone who is loyal to a fault and yet, what was it that left a bad taste in my mouth for God's most beloved creation?

After doing some soul searching and trying to figure out why I felt this way, God revealed to me that I have a strong sense of justice. We all technically do. It wasn't people I didn't like, per se, it was our behavior. Humans are a finicky bunch, and because of my love for people, when someone did me wrong, did someone innocent wrong, someone I loved wrong, I needed them to pay for what they did even in the most minor of circumstances. I didn't understand why common sense was not so common. Like, why can't people just act right?

I realized that although a lot of people won't admit it (especially my fellow Christians), I am in good company. If we delve deep into the root of why we feel so strongly about justice, we will find that because we were made in God's image, it's something, for the most part, a lot of us can't help. Now, whether our ideas of justice are correct and if we go about seeking it in the right way is another story.

If I'm honest, in my ideal world there is immediate payment for each offense. I mean, who wouldn't want a world
like that? In this utopia, all the bad guys immediately get
caught and go to jail for their crimes. Anyone who did something shady, like steal your cookies, would instantly get a
bellyache and throw up said cookie. I know; I did say I was
petty, right?

We would have an ideal society where good triumphs
over evil in every single instance.

All that was good and well until I realized that I was personally not immune to this type of justice. It's pretty funny
how we judge people on their actions and then turn around
and judge ourselves by our intentions. As Christians, we are
challenged to look at what standard we are using to evaluate our justice. How do we evaluate good and evil? How do
we determine what a proper punishment is for an offense?
What bar was set at the foundation of this thing we call life
that determines if we are on the right side?

The answer to that is *perfection*. The standard was set
by and through a holy and perfect God who can never do
any wrong. He can never even have a bad thought and
because He is holy, He cannot accept anything that is not
holy. In other words, sin. The payment for sin is death. Not
just some sin, all sin. Anything that is against a perfect and
holy God is sin and is deserving of the death penalty. So,
stealing that mint ball from that bodega when you were five:
sin. And… guess what that deserves.

No one's acts are righteous in that case, not even one.
Death is the great equalizer. It puts everyone on the same
playing field. We all are deserving of the same sentence no
matter how big or small we may think an offense is.

If we took the time out to look at ourselves, it would destroy us to find out that we are just as dirty as the cookie thief. We would have a change of heart and even hold the cookie thief's hair while they threw up. (Honestly, don't steal my cookies. I still want you to throw it up…God is clearly still working on me).

Ultimately, I had to learn that in God's world, we are all dirty. "There is no righteous person, not even one." (Rom. 3:10) As the Holy Spirit began to work on my heart, I realized my petty nature was something God wanted to use for His glory.

Now hear me out. I know that sounds strange, but the devil is always out here, perverting what God wants of His children.

We Have An Enemy

I'm going to take a second and stop right here. I believe God exists, so, therefore, I trust that His Words in the Bible are accurate and we have an enemy. An enemy who does not want to see us succeed, an enemy who hates us with every ounce of his being, and an enemy who is straight-up trash, for lack of better words. He is the ultimate hater, deceiver, killer, and destroyer of everything. he only seeks to steal, kill and destroy (Jn. 10:10). he is a roach doomed to destruction.

I don't know If you realized it, but I try to make sure all "the roach's" pronouns are lowercase. Why? Because I'm petty, and he is the only one I'm allowed to pulverize. From now on, whenever I speak of the devil, he will be referenced as the roach, pest, or something of that nature, because those disgusting, vile creatures are the ultimate picture of what the devil is. he is beneath us, annoying and nasty. Get it? Got it? Good.

Too many of God's people are afraid of something we have authority over. Something we have the power to trample on its head (Ps. 91:13). A being that, although he used to be with God, is the opposite of God. God, through Jesus, has given us the authority to dispose of the roach and his roachettes, just as He does. Throughout several chapters of this book, I quote an African proverb that reads: "A lion does not turn around when a dog barks". Sometimes the proverb is stated "when a small dog barks". The lion knows that he is a lion, and that he is a threat to his aggressor by simply being who he is. He does not turn around because he knows that although that "little dog" may nip at him, he has already won the fight! It is a reminder that such is the case with us in Christ!

The world has done way too good a job at elevating the fear in people regarding that bug rather than exalting the power of the Most High God. Between movies, books, television, social media, and our own influences from the dark realm, the enemy has invaded the minds of the world and even the chosen people of God, to either convince them that bug is not as bad as he is, make him a joke, make hell seem like a party, or to instill such fear in our hearts that we are too afraid to stand in our God-given authority. he has gotten away with his lies for way too long. Therefore, he must be diminished and put in his place so we can gain the courage to fight like we know we have already won.

MY OWN FEAR

I know of this fear all too well. It's something I have dealt with since as far back as I can remember, even as a small child. I must start by saying that based on evidence in scripture, the roach is not subject to time as we are, and so he may very well be aware of who we will be. he is not omnipresent like God, which is why he needs a lot of help from demons, human agents, our own insecurities, the power of suggestion, time, and even God's own prophecies. That vermin is very well organized (Mt. 12:26). he uses every-thing at his disposal to try to thwart the purposes of God.

We see evidence of this after Jesus' birth, where he influenced Herod to kill all those children:

"16 Then Herod, when he saw that he had been tricked by the wise men, became furious, and he sent and killed all the male children in Bethlehem and in all that region who were two years old or under, according to the time that he had ascertained from the wise men. 17 Then was fulfilled what was spoken by the prophet Jeremiah:
18 "A voice was heard in Ramah,
weeping and loud lamentation,
Rachel weeping for her children;
she refused to be comforted because they are no more."
(Mt. 2:16-18, ESV)

This example shows you that the roach does not care or see innocence; he sees threats. This is just one reason parents need to be covering their children in prayer. He killed all those children looking for one child.

But then again…

That child saved *everyone*!

I mean, I'll give that bug one thing, he is good at being evil. It's all he knows. he's been practicing it for so long, so why wouldn't he be good at it?

Now for me, I have always been sensitive to the spiritual realm. I can't remember everything, but I know I have even had angelic encounters as a kid. However, the enemy would try to scare me through many different means, even from the mouths of those I loved, who had not dealt with their own fear and worry surrounding the supernatural, as well as instances where the roach would fully be trying to intimidate me as a young child.

It's story time.

When I was eight years old, my oldest brother had a room on the top floor in our house where my younger brother and I would play video games and watch TV. Sometimes all of us together and sometimes one-offs. Those days with my brothers on that old-school Super Nintendo were where I learned to whoop people's butts in Street Fighter.

My eldest brother, Guy, heavily trash-talked while playing video games and laughed audibly and loudly at every joke on a TV show. I tell you, he must have missed his calling as a live audience member because his laughs and commentary would have been fantastic for every single 90s sitcom, but I digress. That laugh would always mean he was home and not at work (he is almost twenty years older than my youngest brother and me). Being eight and having no concept of boundaries, I would go upstairs and knock on his door to see what was so funny and spend time with my big brother.

One day, I heard that all too familiar laugh and decided, welp, he's home, let me head upstairs and watch that episode of *Fresh Prince* or whatever he was watching with him. I rushed upstairs, still hearing his laughter, and knocked on his door like I always did. This time, however, he didn't immediately come and unlock his door like usual. I heard his laughter, so I knew he was in there. I knocked one more time and again, with no answer.

Strange.

But I heard him. My attention to detail was impeccable even at that age. So, I looked outside the hallway third-floor window to check for anyone outside. I mean, I did live in the city.

Nope. No one.

But I was sure I heard my brother's laughter, so I walked back over to Guy's bedroom door, and I crouched down to the floor to see if I could see the light from the TV coming from the crack between the floor and the door.

No lights.

But I heard his voice. ***Weird***.

I yelled down the stairs and asked my mom, "Did you see Guy today?" or something of that nature. She yelled back, "He's at work."

Terror took over my entire body.

I ran down those stairs so fast and didn't look back. After that day, I never went upstairs again without calling out my brother's name from the bottom of the steps to make sure he was there and had responded. I don't think he had any idea why I suddenly stopped showing up to his room as usual, but I knew.

That event made me afraid of the roach for a very long time. I concluded that day that if I didn't bother them, they wouldn't bother me. Dumbest thing ever, but that was what the pest wanted. he didn't want me to realize my power in Christ Jesus, because even as young children, we have authority. We are image-bearers, no matter the age. That is why he comes for us so young and pollutes our minds with trash, media, trauma, fear, and anything else he can think of doing. Because he knows if he can mess with us while we are young, we will practice living in fear, sin, greed, hate, and even pettiness. The point being, if he can screw up children, he can make screwed-up adults.

Like I said, the roach is good at being evil.

And much like roaches, when you see one, its friends will soon follow and infiltrate your home if you don't take care of the one you saw.

My husband, Tony has this funny habit I have picked up: when he kills a bug that has entered our home, he leaves it there as an example for the rest. It's silly, but honestly, that's how we have to move with these demons, because that one day took me on a journey of a lifetime trying to fight the fear of the supernatural. Not only did it make me fear the roach and his tactics, but it also took a long time for God to help me realize I was afraid of Him, too. Afraid of anything that had to do with the supernatural at all, even miracles.

I'm a millennial, and I guess to some people, I haven't lived much life, but to give us some credit, we have lived through so much in our short lives, much like Jesus. We have lived through three economic collapses, political unrest, 9/11, and wars. We are the only generation to be poorer than our parents, a whole capitol riot (facepalm), and let's not forget the giant once-every-100-year pandemic elephant in the room, and so much more. And that's just in the U.S.!

That is not to say that our predecessors haven't gone through a lot, but honestly, we don't get the credit we deserve for our resilience. On a personal note, I had a whole baby at the start of this pandemic, but I'll share that story a bit later.

In reality, I have found that there are specific weapons formed for each one of us. The Bible says we have weapons formed against us, which means they are custom-made. Some weapons are even for whole generations. Once we understand that, we can start to fight in a specific way. A way that involves every intricate detail. Even if seemingly trivial. Petty.

For me, the weapon was fear and worry. Fear of the supernatural, and if I was scared of God, how could I have trusted Him to take care of me, or to be a loving father to me?

My fear cultivated worry, because worry happens when you don't believe you have someone to take care of your problems. I didn't know any better, because all I knew around me were people who, on the surface, had a Christian lifestyle but honestly, like most people, didn't trust God. So, if the roach could get me to fear, he could use my already primed environment and triggers he trained into me to raise a worrisome person. And if I was worrisome, I had to take all matters into my own hands, because if I didn't, who would?

I was already someone who innately cared for details, which made the number of things I worried about more significant. And now that I was already worried about everything, why wouldn't every single thing offend me? Why wouldn't I have to take care of it myself?

Do you see where I'm going here?

Now in all this, I had a great family—something like out of the storybooks. I was the only daughter growing up. Both my parents loved each other. We had family dinners, took vacations, spent quality time together, etc. I didn't have to watch Disney Channel to have the family I wanted. However, the picture-perfect family was only surface level. Nothing is truly great without a full relationship with Jesus. No matter how stable your home is, it is like a house built on sand that the ocean could easily sweep up. Le roach, aware of this, hopped on that generational and environmental mistrust in God like a fly landing on your burger at a barbecue.

The roach is *really* good at being evil.

Something he started with me as a child bred a full-blown problem. Again, I can't stress enough how important it is to pray over your children. At the root of every petty, angry, trash-talking person is insecurity. Insecurity in who can take care of them. Mistrust in the one who created them. Mistrust in God.

I say all that to say: of course, the roach would want to pervert my attention to detail. It is the very thing that God placed in me and designed to be used as a weapon against him. Of course, he would want me concerned about getting vengeance on my own vs. letting God deal with every situation. It makes sense that he would like me to believe my worries are too small to bring to God. Of course, the roach would want me to only come to God in emergencies. You know, that moment when I **really** can't figure it out on my own. Of course, he would want me to believe I was in control and I had to be the one to get justice for myself, my loved ones, my friends, etc., on my own. However, remember that all roaches, when you turn on the lights, scatter. When God flipped the switch and I realized my attention to detail, the need for justice in every situation and to get back at an enemy, were a tool God wanted to use in me to war with the darkness, I could begin to see the roach's hand in every single little detail. I could use all the things I noticed, all the anger, and all my past experiences to fight my **real** enemy. Oh snap, roach, **you have been exposed!**

There are so many things in our lives that are seemingly bad habits, in which the enemy has used our ignorance to pervert what God intended to use for His kingdom. That shouldn't come as a surprise, especially because le roach has never changed.

We know God is the same yesterday, today, and tomorrow, but the roach has also stayed the same. He's been a deceiver from the beginning (Jn. 8:44), and if we really look at it, he hasn't changed either. Which means if we pay attention, we can see his tricks coming from a mile away. This is another reason distraction is one of his main weapons against us.

The fact that he hasn't changed is just another way he tries to be like God and yet always falls oh so short. Why? Because he's a roach. Let me stop. No, but really, let's take a step back and think of the rudest person you have ever met. Someone who has serious anger issues, a liar, a thief, whatever the problem is. Hey, maybe that person is you.

That energy was meant for the devil and his minions. Angry person, you were meant to be a warrior. Liar, you were meant to be creative, to tell stories that bring people to the Lord. And even you, thief, you were created to **rob Hell!**

Now if the roach can get you to use the gifts God has given you for spiritual warfare on people rather than him, he has destroyed what God intended for your life.

A lot of Christians may think anger is a bad thing, but God gets angry. Remember that time He sent like a whole host of people straight to Hell? Look in the book of Numbers (Nb. 16:22). It's a crazy thing. But if we are made in His image, why wouldn't we also get angry? The Bible says to be angry and do not sin (Ep.4:26). Nowhere does it say never to get angry. Why? Because we're supposed to. We're supposed to be angry when we see the roach destroying someone's destiny. We are supposed to get offended at the schemes of the enemy. We are supposed to be upset and war with the devil. Why? Because we are warriors! Holy anger is of God. Our weapons are not carnal, but that passion is because we are supposed to be fighters.

Just imagine all that energy for the kingdom. If that same person would put on righteous armor, pick up their sword and battle to the death, they would be a force to be reckoned with. Why wouldn't that pest want you distracted by being angry with fellow image bearers?

COFFEE BREAK

Periodically, I will insert coffee break sections in order to share some personal experiences, article's I have written and/or ask some seemingly probing questions connected to the chapter we are on. This is to encourage introspection as well as explore the depths of God's power and love. I'm not going to lie: these questions and stories are confronting and will get in your business as the good Lord often does with me. The good news is that you can share the answers to those questions to as little or as many people as possible. But always as the Lord leads. Now let's get started with some questions:

1. How have you been petty today? Yesterday? Last month? Last year? 5 seconds ago?
2. Why? Was it worth it?
3. Who got hurt? Did you apologize?
4. Finally, How do you see God changing your behavior for His glory?

Petty with a Capital P

Purpose

A Lion does not turn around when a dog barks"~
African Proverb

Sons and Daughters of God

O n a spiritual, physical, emotional, and everything level, we are connected to God in ways we can never understand, even if we choose to ignore it. It is the result of being made in His image. We were intricately designed with a purpose to be mini examples of God on Earth. The best model I can find to explain the term "made in His image" can be found in the way we relate to our earthly parents.

We are all images of our fathers and mothers who came before us. Even if we are adopted, separated at birth, or don't even like our parents, we tend to look like them physically, biologically, emotionally, speak similarly, and have similar tastes, etc. Unfortunately, we may also have similar vices and predispositions to illnesses. It's why siblings who were separated as children (or twins at birth) will come together and find out they have similar behaviors and have made similar life choices. It's also why you may have to make that awkward phone call to your parents from the doctor's office to find out if Grandma Betsy had a history of diabetes.

We are genetically predisposed to being a certain way, whether in body or behavior. We can choose different paths in actions and pray against generational disease, however, some things cannot be helped. It is the way we were created. The image is ingrained in every part of our DNA. In everyone and everything's DNA. Heck, your dog was made in the image of his parents. Such is the case with God and us.

Love and holiness are God's nature. Think of this as what He looks like. He can't help it. It's who He is. In the same way we can't help our race or gender, or the fact that we are human beings, God can't help being holy and loving. Because He is holy, He must be a just judge and love justice. It comes with the package. (Ps. 37:28)

Subsequently, as God's image bearers, deep down, people want to be holy. It's in our spiritual DNA. But we have a problem: sin. Our flesh is evil. And that flesh…. really likes being evil.

Just like we resemble our Heavenly Father in spirit, our flesh is like our physical fathers, and without God, we simply cannot help but be evil. Sure, we may want to be better and strive for better behavior, but ultimately, this duality causes a war within ourselves that can only be won by devoting our lives to Christ.

Our sin separates us from our holy and loving God because our nature no longer mirrors His own. Sin can be compared to a horrific accident in which we have been left with amnesia and are no longer recognizable even to our own parents. This parent being our Heavenly Father.

Furthermore, because we have no memory of them, even when our family comes to claim us, we don't believe them because we now identify with a similarly mangled imposter who has convinced us that we are his, even though our DNA says otherwise. What a tragic state of affairs!

Thankfully, even though we were broken, and battered, with no idea whose we are or where we were going, God made a way out of our torment and reconciled our broken relationship through Jesus. The picture of Jesus' battered body on the cross not only symbolizes judgment but also symbolizes the current state of humanity. Christ's payment for our sin not only grants us the right to be adopted into God's family, but He also promises to erase all our sin and heal all our wounds if we just accept Him. It is only through Christ that we can be reclaimed, and both legally and naturally become sons and daughters of God.

In the beginning, everything was perfect. We were perfect. God's purpose for us was to walk with Him forever. His intention from the start was to bless people generationally, to spread His holy image throughout the Earth. We are His most prized creation. Unfortunately, as a result of the fall we were separated from being one with God and fully representing His likeness, and we started making defective copies. I know that sounds a bit rough, but that's what sin does. It creates outlet store products... you know, when the stitching is just a little off. I mean, it has the name, but there's a reason why it's discounted.

We desire to move apart from God and as we can see by the state of this world, walking apart from God is not a good idea. However, just like the outlet store products, this fact does not negate our very created existence and the laws He set in motion. Gucci is still Gucci.

The laws God set in place still move in us because He spoke them into existence and His Word never comes back void (Isa. 55:1). It is just tainted by sin, which leads to the mess we are in today. While righteousness breeds generational blessings, sin results in generational curses. That worm knows this, and like the disgusting creep he is, he takes advantage of this all the time. Since he's a poser and always wants to be like God, he wants children of his own. Our sin, through our coupled actions and unrepentant hearts, caused us to identify the roach as our father because sin came from him.

There are literally only two options. Good or evil. If we're not moving according to the image of God, who is all things good, and if everything apart from God is evil, then we can only be sons and daughters of the originator of sin. I don't know about you, but I refuse to be the child of a maggot.

Since sin is a poison that has infiltrated our physical DNA, these two opposite states of being will be in a royal rumble until the day the Lord returns. Take it from Paul himself (you know, the guy who wrote half the New Testament): *"I do not understand what I do. For what I want to do I do not do, but what I hate I do."* (Rom. 7:15, NIV)

Now, as redeemed sons and daughters of God through the sacrifice of Jesus, we have been reconciled to Him. He promises to remember our sins no more. Once we accept Jesus into our lives, He counts all our good deeds and washes all our sins away with His blood, even the ones we still struggle with. What a scandal! He gave us the ultimate cheat sheet. We can come to Him with any and every single thing, like children do to their parents.

I know a lot of us may feel grown up and that we can do things ourselves, and have made God an afterthought or backup for our own strength, but y'all, that is not the relationship God wants with us. We are missing out on something truly beautiful if we are too proud to go to God with our troubles, even for the smallest things.

Our purpose is to dwell with God. Adam and Eve walked with Him in the cool of the day. They were naked and unashamed. It wasn't until they started to want to provide for themselves and to basically be their own gods that things went astray. If we can recognize that all the provision God gave to Adam and Eve in the garden is now available to us, we would walk and talk differently. Sure, things are different than the garden, since evil exists in this world, but the provision is still the same. He promises to take care of all our needs. **All!**

Sons and Daughters

So you see, although we are made in God's image, God's definition for His children is different than just having His face. Take it from people who were adopted and were truly given a better life. God's intention was that children mirror their fathers and mothers in all things good, just as Jesus mirrored His Heavenly Father on Earth. (Jn. 14:9)

Jesus moved through this Earth in power and in dependence all at the same time. He was in full submission and had all authority. The words I have used may seem like opposites, but we serve a God who can do two seemingly very different things at the same time. It is the paradox of God. He wants us to surrender victoriously. He wants full dependence on Him while knowing that the power of the Holy Spirit dwells within us, knowing we can do all things through Him but can do nothing apart from Him (Jn. 15:5). That is what it means to be a child of God.

My Struggle With Dependence

Gifted

I have struggled with depending on anyone for anything my entire life. I was raised by two super proud Caribbean parents, and on top of that, I was considered "gifted" my entire life.

As a "gifted" child, I potty trained myself, was speaking full sentences as a one-year-old, and started reading entire books at age three, among other things my parents will never let me forget. When my mother saw I had a drive for learning, she taught me at home, as I was too young to be in school and she was not a fan of daycare. By the time I entered pre-school, the teachers all told my parents I "acted like an adult." I was placed in something called the Eagle program that next year in kindergarten.

The Eagle program was a program for children who are "elite" in public schools. We were considered the smartest. We were separated to a certain extent from the rest of the school. We were taught an advanced curriculum, and this was basically like a private school setting inside of a public school. There was a top class and there was a second best, and in all honesty, I barely saw any other kids. We actually only crossed paths with the second best class on the special trips that only the first two classes were allowed to go on.

I spent the entirety of my elementary school career in the Eagle class. I got all A's, or should I say E's for Excellent. Around the fifth grade, I started to let my grades slip. I was more interested in friends than I was in my studies. Needless to say, my parents were **not** happy. I didn't fail, I just didn't put as much effort in that year, and who knew a lazy year when I was ten would send me on a spiral of never feeling good enough?

Because of that year, I was not in the smartest class in junior high, but was still in the special programs, which now spread the "elite" children across six classes. I may have slacked in fifth grade, but they couldn't deny the gift God placed in me. Meanwhile, my strict Caribbean parents put a lot of pressure on me to do better in junior high. I had always gotten above 90 percent on everything in school, and anything lower from me was tantamount to blasphemy.

I worked my hardest and ended up upgrading a class and getting eight awards by junior high graduation. The announcers even asked my mother to stay standing, as there were many awards coming and they didn't want her to have to keep getting up and sitting down. I was proud of myself, as I never really needed help from anyone to accomplish my schoolwork. I just got it done. In high school, fifth grade happened all over again. I met the man who would become my husband, had a lot of friends, and my schoolwork, although still a driving force behind my self-esteem, took a back seat. Think about this: I was a kid in AP classes who didn't take school seriously. (Facepalm.) I remember one class, I only showed up for the review and the tests and got above ninety on all my tests. The teacher, I guess, realized I was just bored, and literally said to me one time, "See you next test?" At which I laughed, and she only took off 5 percent for my attendance and I got a ninety in that class.

This may seem like a lot of personal information for no reason, but I assure you, I have a point. My identity was based around what I could achieve my entire life. My jobs, my marriage, and college have all followed suit and have all been performance-driven on my part, and the cycles just kept on repeating. Literally.

When I fell short because of, I don't know, being a kid, or being bored, or what have you, I was penalized. So, I worked harder for the approval of my parents and everyone around me. When I was diagnosed with MS and had to leave a great, high-paying, performance-driven job, it broke me. I could no longer do it for myself. I had to depend on people.

Of course, I was broken. It was important that I "acted like an adult" at all times. That was my identity. And when I fell short of that identity in any way, which I was always bound to do because I was born broken with sin, instead of asking for help, I just strived to do more and more, which inevitably caused burnout. In my eyes, being an adult or a child who behaved like one meant I could do things by myself. That was what I was praised for and therefore, if I fell short, that was what I ran to. To do things on my own.

Now, how can a person who thinks success means doing it by yourself truly understand what it means to depend on God? How could I accept such a giant gift for free?

When Jesus found me, I was excited not to have to worry about everything, but putting it into practice was not easy. I treated God like my boss. Legalism is birthed out of this mindset, and I must admit, as much as I had zeal for God and truly wanted to be better, it was a struggle to leave my achievement mindset behind. In all honesty, it dawned on me just recently how much being labeled gifted and not living up to what society expects of you makes you feel like a failure. Trust me, I have a lot of friends who were right there with me in those classes, and we all have shared trauma, even my own brother. But what a relief the gospel is. God knows we are preconditioned to fail, and He loves us anyway. He doesn't want us to work for it, He just wants us to trust Him, and He will do the work in us.

I spent my entire life striving for a goal that had no destination or fruit. This is the reason why people who have "made it" in the eyes of the world can still be so discontented. God is the author of our purpose, and no amount of work, intelligence, or money can buy it. It's already ours. We just have to believe.

God allowed me to achieve all my great achievements in life not by being qualified, but being called. It was by design. My father, whom I love dearly, is also an extremely intelligent man, but lord knows that smart people can be so smart they're dumb to what's sitting right in front of them. God wanted something different for me. He allowed all that transpired to keep me humble while using my gifts for His glory... not mine.

God is a Person

Just like us, God is a person. The three persons of the Trinity. I want to explain how all this works, but I'm human, and in all honesty, if I could explain God, we would be here all millennia. There are not enough books in the world to count what Jesus did on Earth (Jn. 21:25), let alone explain the all-powerful God. In an attempt to explain how we relate to His image, I like to look at God represented as a body and a family at the same time.

This family is made up of the Father (soul: mind/personality/emotion), Son (body) and the Holy Spirit (spirit). Just like most of us in our families tend to have the same last name, the name that unites them is God. It's what identifies us and them as being part of a package. Our souls, bodies, and spirits also come in a package, which is us. Each person of the Trinity is perfectly equal in essence and all God, who allows us to call them "He," since, let's be honest, we tend to be stupid and He just kept it simple. In the same way our body, soul, and spirit inhabit one vessel and we are called by our names, He (the Trinity) also inhabits one vessel. The vessel of the Godhead functions perfectly in unison and has different roles, much like why your eyes, nose, and ears have different jobs, and also how God intended marriage and the family unit to be.

> **For this reason a man will leave his father and mother and be united to his wife, 8 and the two will become one flesh.' So they are no longer two, but one flesh. 9 Therefore what God has joined together, let no one separate. (Mk. 10:7-9)**

I even take it a step further to say that God meant for each member of the family to represent a specific member of the Godhead. Men represent the Father, women represent the Holy Spirit, and we all represent Jesus as the Son. It's why the Bible says, "Let us make mankind in *our* image" (Gen. 1:26). It's pretty trippy that God can represent your body, a family, your soul, and your spirit all at once. It's complex and simple all at the same time, but I'm just going to leave this here because I don't know about you, but I don't have all millennia.

These are just a few examples of how He can be one God and three persons all at the same time and why He is the ultimate loving family. You want a father, you have a Heavenly Father, you need a mother, you have the nurturing of the Holy Spirit, and you have a brother in Christ.

We need to start relating to God as a member of our family and as the all-powerful God all at the same time. A lot of us, myself included, struggle with the idea that a being so powerful would want to relate to us in this way, and that we could have a family, because the term "family" has been loaded for us by bad Christ representatives. I'll talk a little more about this later.

God is Petty

So now that we've established that God is a person, we can start assigning attributes of personhood to Him. I know this may sound like elementary stuff, but being "too smart for my own good," I didn't understand this and I know that I'm in good company.

It wasn't until I really started getting into the Word that the Holy Spirit guided me to things I could not have understood just reading the Bible at face value. There are so many descriptions of His character, His nature, how loving He is, and evidence in His actions that solidify that we are dealing with a petty God!

Let's get back to meaning of petty, shall we? **Petty means: Of little importance, trivial.** But to whom? Who decides what is of little importance? Who makes the decision that something is not important enough to care about, and from whom did they get the authority to decide such a thing over your life? What's important to me may not be important to you, but does that mean it's not important?

Does a consensus from the majority even mean that something is not important?

God says in His Word that he "numbers the hairs on our heads" (Lk. 12:7). Like what? He's talking about the throwaway hairs, you know, the ones that go in the trash. Every. Single. Day. Like 100 of them every single day. **He counts those!** We don't even count those, and they're on our own bodies. Those hairs are important to God and not one of them falls out without Him knowing about it.

That's crazy!

So if God (you know, the guy who created the stars, the moon, all the animals, you know literally **All. The. Things**.) cares about something that is thrown away, why wouldn't your cares matter to Him?

So I ask you, as image bearers, if we have feelings, can God have feelings? I don't know about you, but my crazy Caribbean family had all the feelings. After all, they are people. Think about all the attributes it takes to be human. Now think about that on a grander scale: that is God. Obviously, without sin, but you get the picture.

Do you ever wonder why we have an enemy? Why that cockroach hates us so much? Simple: because he's a hater, but also what is the reason? Haters hate because they are jealous of something. Now what can the roach possibly be jealous of?

Bible Story Time

I used to watch a tv show called "The Golden Girls" where an elderly character named Sophia would say "Picture This" whenever she was about to tell a long-winded story from the past. I promise not to be too long-winded but, allow me to go into a quick Bible montage "Golden Girls" style.

Picture this…

Heaven, like before all of the things. God, whom we've established is the Father, Son, and Holy Spirit, is in heaven ruling all the things in perfection. Joy is all over the place, there are angels, the streets are made of gold, plants are alive, literally everything is alive down to the colors, and the gold itself. I mean, why not? It's God's house, and He is the author of life.

Everything He has created is perfect and His creation serves Him out of love because they see who He is and how He takes care of them. Everyone has a job, a place to stay and live in the abundance that is God's world.

Now there is one angel whom He placed right under the Godhead. Right after Jesus Himself. His name was Lucifer. God broke the mold when He made him. The Bible says he was the most beautiful thing God ever created. Not only that, he was in charge of so much in God's kingdom. It wasn't long before all this beauty, fame, and trust from the other angels started to get to his head.

He became so conceited that he started to think he was better than God, and he could do a better job at running the universe. [2]

Bananas!

This is when Lucifer officially became the roach we know today. Sin originated in his heart, and he started to spread that virus like a cancer to the other angels. I don't know if he was just dumb or stupid, but sin tends to make you lose your whole mind somewhere. In all honesty, **how could he not think God knew?!**

---

[2] "Lucifer's Fall from Heaven - Youtube." Accessed December 5, 2021. https://www.youtube.com/watch?v=DNcGVAk5I0I.

God even tried to warn him, and that centipede carried on, infecting the other angels. He used the trust and rapport with the other angels that he had gained during his time serving God to deceive them into thinking God was somehow unfair and that he would do a better job at running things. Think about it: up until this point, these angels didn't know what sin was. Y'all, he infected one-third of God's angels with his propaganda. Honestly, I don't know about you, but I feel a lot better knowing that we were not the first ones out here getting tricked.

Now that being said, we all know how the story ends. Michael, God's right hand man, warred against him with the remaining two-thirds of the angels, and le roach and all his roachettes, get kicked out of heaven and sent to Hell, where he officially becomes satan the accuser. he becomes the picture of evil. So you see, Hell was created for the devil and his angels. Sin must be punished because we serve a holy God. God doesn't want us to go there because it wasn't made for us, but we actually send ourselves there by being kin to the roach in sin.

Here's where it gets interesting. We all know what happened in the garden. Adam was created and told to protect the garden. Why? Because there was someone lurking, not only to try to gain more company in hell but to gain the kingdom he always wanted. When God created Eve, Adam was immediately in love with her and he basically onboarded her to life in the garden and told her the one rule: "You can have everything in this garden, just don't eat from that one tree." For a while, they lived in bliss, being one with God. Having dominion over all of God's earthly creation. Y'all, God gave to us what the roach wanted to take from Him.

Wouldn't you know it? The hater of all things good slithered into the garden and persuaded Eve to eat the forbidden fruit. That insect already knew that Eve's information was given to her by Adam, so he stirred up doubt in her heart, not only about God but for her husband's leadership. He specifically targeted God's order and goodness, making God seem unfair, just like he did with the fallen angels.

I know a lot of people would ask: Why would God even put that tree in the garden in the first place? Here it is: God is not a robot keeper. He rules in love and not in control. He wants you to be able to choose to love and serve him, and with that choice must come a choice not to love and serve Him. It must exist so that free will exists. He knows that He knows best, but His love language is trust. And trusting Him helps you serve Him.

Let's get back to the roach in the Garden. The Bible says the snake was the craftiest of all the animals. The word crafty, like the word petty, also has many negative connotations in culture but if you really look at some of its positive meanings it means: calculating, sharp, cunning, adeptness in performance, dexterity, appealing, etc. So if God made the snake and it was good when He made it, there was nothing wrong with its nature until it was used by the devil (Gen. 1:25).

Think about it, Adam and Eve's first job was to name the animals. They **named it**, so they knew it. The roach chose an animal that was appealing, skillful, and calculating, and also had a familiar face that Adam and Eve already trusted.

Y'all, does that not sound familiar? Think about that the next time a family member is driving you nuts or when you yourself are driving someone you love up a wall. He used the exact same trick he used on the angels in heaven. We all know what happened next: Eve ate the fruit and handed it to Adam, who was standing literally right there, watching the snake convince his wife to disobey God, and then ate it **himself**! Think about it: Eve heard it from Adam, and Adam heard it from God Himself before Eve was even created. Check your timeline. It's the reason that God only called Adam when He arrived in the garden. He was the one held responsible for guarding the garden.

In the end, Adam and Eve were offered something that was already theirs to begin with and their dominion was stolen from them. Since the roach couldn't steal authority from God, he stole it from us and just like that, Adam and Eve were kicked out of paradise, mirroring what happened to the roach in Heaven, but this time a kingdom was stolen.

Now here's the kicker: when we got kicked out, God didn't throw us away. He promised to save us and continues to bless us. He loves us and didn't cause immediate death, and allowed us to get back in right standing with Him through Jesus.

The Hater

The creation and fall of humanity display our petty God in action. He basically paraded what the roach wanted in his face, with beings less than him in power and stature. Nothing gets someone who is jealous of you angrier than when you are favored, while believing you're not good enough for what you have. Ask Jesus. Think about it: the Bible says He made us out of dust, so basically, God gave dirt authority over the roach. Dirt! Oh, how I love my petty God!

But God has chosen the foolish things of the world to put to shame the wise, and God has chosen the weak things of the world to put to shame the things which are mighty. (1 Cor. 1:27, NKJV)

God wanted to show all His creation on Earth and in Heaven what He can do with "the least of these." He chose to make our frame from something so humble, and lower than the angels (Ps. 8:5), and yet make us powerful through our relationship with Him.

Here lies the main reason the roach is a hater. God made a way out for us through Jesus. In fact, it was satan himself who influenced the hearts of those who had Jesus killed. Not only did God withhold redemption from him, He allowed the roach's own evil to be his destruction. And just like that, at the resurrection, dominion was ripped from his hands. **Ouch! That must sting.**

I mean, why should God provide a way out for him? The roach was in Heaven with God. He saw God in His full glory and still decided to rebel. Honestly, that always boggled my mind. he saw God in all His glory and power and thought he could take Him on. he probably mistook God's kindness for weakness and believed God was so loving that He would just hand over the throne, which is even more idiotic. I read that somewhere, and honestly, it makes sense.

Not only did he rebel, but he also took a third of God's angels with him. So the stupidity makes copies. If that doesn't sound like humans, I don't know what does.

I firmly believe we are capable of the same, and that's why God doesn't dwell here. He is protecting us from ourselves. Furthermore, it's dirty here. If I were God, I wouldn't want to be on Earth anymore either. It's a ghetto. I'm just glad He didn't throw us in the trash and start over, because that's what He should have done, I mean, He did do it once with the flood. Do you ever thank God for what He doesn't do? But all jokes aside, God sent His own Son down to this ghetto to get killed for the dirt that we did! If that's not loving, I don't know what is. And His Son said, "Sure, Dad!" and did it! If I were Jesus, my response would have probably been, "Dad, You want Me to leave the streets of gold to do what?... and go where?" But Jesus is also God, so it doesn't surprise me.

The rule of Hell was created before we existed, but the scandal is that God created a second death. Death is eternal separation from God, but He made a physical death to take the place of ultimate separation. In reality, what is called the second death (going the Hell) was supposed to be the first one, but God put a stepping block in between this physical life and eternity, not just as judgement but to give us a second chance and a future. I believe that Adam and Eve didn't immediately physically die because their bodies had to learn how to, because they were created to live forever like God. Many people miss this, but physical death is God's grace to humanity. You see, God had a plan from the beginning.

Physical death is a reminder that we will someday meet our Maker and die with Christ on the cross. Jesus paved the way for everlasting life so that even we, as dirty as we are, can have eternal life.

The roach seriously hates that we have a second chance. Also, his time is running out, and his only real goal is to get as much company in his misery as possible. We all know the saying, "Misery likes company," and unfortunately, that termite has an abundance of it.

In essence, the roach is petty too. But just like his pronouns in this book, he's petty with a lowercase p. If he can find any little thing to cause us discomfort or mess with our joy and contentment, he will do it. Outside of the massively horrible stuff that the pest does, there are so many minor annoyances that, when added up, cause us to change our thinking or mood, even if just for that day. Just think about the last time you were in a traffic jam (traffic jams are straight from le roach), the last time someone (even someone you loved) said that one thing that set you off after having a great day. It was seemingly minor, but it was the last straw. Isn't it crazy how the very things we love can be used against us? Huh, it sounds like a pest to me. Just think about that nasty fly that tries to get into your food at the barbecue, and better yet, those mosquitos. I honestly have found no purpose for mosquitos in this world, outside of reminding us to stay saved. I honestly believe their eternal home is the fiery pit.

But we can be Petty with a capital P because ours stands for Purpose. There is a grander purpose to depending on God for everything. Every time something bothers us, we take it to God. Many people wouldn't pray that fly away, but I would. It breeds dependency on the one who is the owner of everything. Think about it: if the devil could use that fly to annoy you, why not use that same fly to remind him whose you are? Now, that's the type of Petty I'm talking about. Do you know that God cares about that prayer just as much as He cares about you praying for someone on their death bed?

Pettiness is a Battle Strategy

God's Word says to "cast **all** your cares on him, for he cares for you." (1 Pet. 5:7,NKJV) I believe it says that because if we can practice on the fly, or on a rainy day when you're trying not to get your hair wet after going to the hair salon (true story, God stopped the rain for me), we will have the faith built up to pray fervently for someone who is on their deathbed.

How can we activate resurrection faith on a whim? Jesus showed the disciples many miracles that had nothing to do with raising people from the dead. He had to build their trust and give them examples of His miracles.

Think about it, Jesus' first miracle basically saved someone's party. He literally made wine because people ran out. Given there are always reasons and hidden messages in His miracles. For example, in this miracle He turned something seemingly basic into something amazing, much like He does with our lives. But to be real... the only thing the guests at the wedding knew was that there wasn't wine and now there was. ***Party was still on!*** Y'all, God saved somebody's party. He cares about **everything**!

Now, we are human, and when Jesus was crucified, it's likely in the moment the disciples forgot all the things He did, but when He was raised from the dead after dying the death that He did for our sins, they could use all those other miracles as reference points for when times got hard. The disciples were imprisoned, beaten, flogged, and even died for the faith. Why? Because they had hope in His saving grace, His care for their every need, and in His resurrection power. Their hope was not only on the things Jesus did but on the miracles that God performed through them and for them, even in the tiniest of details.

As citizens of a first world country, we have become so comfortable that we have forgotten God's power and have become so dependent on man. Some of the most enormous faith I have seen comes from people who have been persecuted. Believers worldwide have to pray to eat and survive for their faith, and a lot of us won't even bring Jesus up in a conversation because it's not politically correct. With all the love in my heart, who cares about political correctness when we serve the Author of truth? The most transformative revivals are happening in the middle of places that no one seems to care about, even in this country, because in those places, no one has time for political correctness. **They need miracles!**

Once we get into the practice of praying for smaller things, they become huge catalysts for building the faith posture needed for extraordinary miracles. He goes by the measure of your faith. **Have big faith!**

COFFEE BREAK

Hi, grab a coffee or something else to drink, heck grab a noisy snack and really think about the following questions:

1. What minor or not so minor annoyances has the roach been using to get under your skin?
2. How can you use those minor annoyances to show him whose you are?
3. Lastly, name one way you can be petty with a capital P today.

God Cares

He's a Good Father

"A Lion does not turn around when a dog barks"
~ African Proverb

As much as that creepy-crawler tries to convince you otherwise: God cares about you!

He cared so much for you that He sent His only Son to die for you. I need to make this personal. He died for you personally. He died for you, sitting in your house, your car, the one who lives at that address, the one who did all those reckless things a couple of years ago, and yes, the one who did that reckless stuff two seconds ago. He loves you no matter what you do and wants to be reconciled with you. He loves each and every one of us as if we each were His only child, and gave up His only Son for us while we didn't even want a relationship with Him. Personally, that is the craziest thing I've ever heard. He basically hugs us as we spit in His face. Imagine a love like that.

Let me paint a better picture. He didn't have to create us, but He did. Think about it. He chose to call us His bride even though He knew we would cheat on Him every single day. How many people would do that? He knew we would always struggle, knew it would always be a problem for us, yet still died for our sins and accepts us back each time we ask for forgiveness.

He loves us past our faults, protects us, gives us joy, provides for us, and makes us well even though we don't deserve it. We were blood bought by God Himself. The Creator of the universe gave His life for us. So next time that skunk tries to pollute your mind with that "I'm not worthy" stench, and tries to convince you that you are anything but loved by God, remind him that you are expensive and that he… well… is a thrown-out has-been.

I know love that big can be intimidating for a lot of us, myself included. It's hard to accept that kind of love, especially since the best way anyone can love you on this Earth is already tainted by brokenness.

Our relationship with God tends to be colored by our experiences with parents, past relationships, past experiences, and especially bad Christ representatives. No matter who you are, someone who was supposed to love you has wronged you. It's an unfortunate side effect of this broken world and a tactic of that vermin to get you to miss the giant love that is available to you.

Bad Christ Representatives

Let's face it, a lot of us have hang-ups about love and it is simply because we haven't been loved well. We have daddy issues, mommy issues, pastor issues, husband issues, wife issues, friend issues, and every other issue with someone who was supposed to love us well but didn't. And when God calls Himself our Father, that statement is loaded. Loaded with all the trauma we've experienced with our earthly fathers or some authority figure who didn't love us well.

Unfortunately, in one way or another, we have all fallen victim to bad representatives of Christ. And if we are being truthful, we have ourselves been imperfect portrayals of Christ at some point. I know I have. No one is exempt from the fact that we are broken, and unfortunately, we will remain broken until the day Jesus comes back to fix this. And because we are broken, everyone and I mean **everyone**, can and may fail you in some way. We are all capable of it.

Our Parents

The design for humanity was to learn God's ways from the people who bore us because of their own relationship with God and carry that trend through the generations. Our parents have the greatest impact on us based on the design for their role in our lives. So, it stands to reason that our relationships with them can make or break a lot of aspects in our spiritual walks. If our parents are our biggest source of disappointment, that has the greatest impact on how we view God.

To be fair, as a new mother I can tell you that most parents are clueless. The only advantage we have as Christians is that the Word of God is our guide. And what an advantage it is! In His Word, God gives us a blueprint on how to raise our children. Unfortunately for a lot of us, our parents kind of chucked that map right out of the car window and decided to wing it. Christians included. Many times, parents are clouded by culture, their own trauma, and even narcissistic ideations.

When the people responsible for "training us up" in the way that we should go are not following the very person who has all the answers, it will always fail. The roach hops all over that and tries everything in his power to create people filled with trauma in an attempt to thwart what God meant for their lives. Outside of God, the only help we have is either from those same broken people who raised us, YouTube from more broken people, or some other source that can never live up to God's standards.

The good thing is that although we ourselves are not perfect, if we strive to be like Jesus, we will always do better than we would have without Him. Also, if advice is biblically sound, we can take it as the Holy Spirit leads us.

As I said, I had a good family, kind of like the movies. My parents loved each other, all my brothers, and me, but even though in many aspects they were good, there were some very, very broken pieces that caused my mistrust in God. My father has spent his whole life searching for God. Even when he found Him, it was hard for him to accept because his own father was a terrible Christ representative himself. Without spreading too much of my dad's business, his childhood was not good. It had a lot of pain and anguish from people who claimed to know the Lord. It colored his entire life and even his parenting. He swore not to be like his parents, and he wasn't, but he spent his whole life doubting God because of bad Christ representatives, and by example he trained me to do so as well.

My dad was finicky spiritually, so when God called Himself my "Father," that statement was loaded with the attribute of spiritual mistrust. Even when I decided to follow Christ, I found myself apologizing to God on so many occasions because I treated Him like my earthly father. I behaved as though He was finicky, back and forth in what He believed, and that I couldn't depend on Him spiritually.

It was so dumb because God is the Spirit, and I didn't trust Him to be SPIRIT-ually stable (facepalm).

It was especially hard for me to even recognize there was a problem, because it wasn't obvious. My father wasn't abusive, tried his best, worked hard, provided to the best of his ability, so while on the surface I have a great father, God showed me that I needed more: **That He was more.**

I don't know what you've been through with your parents. Some things may even be too horrible for some of you to think about, but I want to let you know that we all have some sort of parental trauma. At some point, our parents scarred us forever, even in the best of situations. Just know that God is there to pick up the pieces and be the Father you always needed. And get this: He knows how to love you in the way you **need** to be loved. He knows your love language. He created it. Trust that He means it when He says He cares.

Abusive Spiritual Leaders

Our parents were broken when we got them and the same is true of our spiritual leaders, in essence our spiritual parents who are also responsible for training us up in the way that we should go. The Bible calls new Christians babies who need milk to eventually become mature enough to eat solid food (Heb. 5:14). But what happens when the milk never runs out or the solid food is rotten (1 Cor. 3:2)?

Sadly, church hurt among Christians is extremely common. I believe this is one of the reasons the Word says not to call anyone father. (Mt. 23:9) This verse is not saying that people don't hold father positions in your life (obviously, because we have earthly fathers and fathers in faith). It is saying that no one should have the position in your heart that rightfully belongs to God, even if that person is a spiritual leader.

Unfortunately, for too many Christians there are spiritual leaders who are placed in the position of God in their hearts regardless of fault. Like I always say, God will not allow anything in His place. He knows He is the only one suited for that position in your heart. I believe that is why in this present time, many spiritual leaders are being exposed as corrupt. (1 Pet. 4:17)

We are all capable of sin, and unfortunately there is a misconception at times that a pastor or clergymen or someone of faith is incapable of doing wrong. Many times, it's placed there by that very same leader to protect themselves, or in our own hearts because we truly want that father we didn't have. **Again, God is that father you didn't have.**

This mindset in the church is evident in the way we handle the things that come out about spiritual leaders. God is a jealous God, and He will rip right out whatever person, place, or thing that is in His place. He is jealous for His position in your heart, and rightfully so, because anything else in God's place leads to destruction. This is especially evident when we find out that people we thought were upstanding turn out to have a lot of skeletons in their closets.

There has been a lot of abuse at the very place where God gathers His flock. I want to get one thing straight: we are the Church. A building and a pastor are not who we are depending on come Judgement Day.

Unfortunately, the signs that a church is toxic is not always obvious from the start. Sometimes it takes years and even decades to recognize that you have been abused spiritually, especially because the perpetrators themselves may or may not even know they are abusive. Toxicity not only has become normalized in homes, but also in the church. Here are some signs that you may be in a toxic church environment:

Signs of a Toxic Church

1. The church is centered around a "charming, charismatic, intense, persuasive, and intelligent personality" who holds unquestioned influence over the congregation as well as being the ultimate spokesperson on all spiritual issues rather than leading people to God.
2. Leadership is not held to the same standard of morality as the rest of the congregation. The leaders' sins are minimized while the people's sins are maximized.
3. Force and intimidation are used by leadership under the guise of honor, respect and authority.
4. No accountability or a facade of accountability (lack of oversight and having yes men as their "accountability": Isolated accountability structure).
5. You cannot disagree with the leadership without repercussions; unsafe environment when dealing with problems, no room for healthy debate over issues.
6. Speaking about private matters or conversations in the pulpit as retaliation (directly or indirectly).
7. Threatened removal under the guise of division
8. Unhealthy focus on wealth and blessings   ·
9. Shunning
10. Purity of doctrine is considered more important than love
11. Busyness and focus on activities
12. Unrealistic promises
13. Fear and shame are used to drive people into submission.

14. Over-spiritualizing (false prophecy used to benefit themselves)
15. Under-spiritualizing (refusing to deal with our spiritual battles). Minimizing the spiritual aspect of our battle and focusing solely on behavior modification.
16. Hovering over personal decisions in a person's life
17. Strong legalistic and religious pressure
18. Denial of the spiritual gifts of the people because the leader must be the first link to God
19. Focus on loyalty to the pastor over loyalty to God[3]

The items on this list are by no means exclusive as there are many other red flags not listed here. Unfortunately, my husband and I have been victims of this type of abuse. Many of the things on this list are things we went through. The crazy thing is, it sneaks up on you. No one willingly decides they want to get abused, at least for the most part. It's something that tends to creep up on you in doses, especially when the perpetrators are supposed to know better, have a good interview face or changed over the course of your time at the church. I was literally asked once why God would speak to the children before He speaks to the father. At that point, I knew this was unhealthy.

I thank God for His sovereignty and for showing me His grace, especially in my weak moments, because many people don't get to a place where they can even remotely

---

[3] Signs of a Toxic Church (Ref: "Have You Noticed These 14 Warning Signs of Spiritual Abuse?" Charisma Magazine. Accessed December 4, 2021. https://www.charismamag.com/spirit/spiritual-growth/33517-have-you-noticed-these-14-warning-signs-of-spiritual-abuse. Accessed December 3, 2021) (Ref: UpChurch, John. "10 Signs of an Abusive Church." Crosswalk.com. Crosswalk.com, May 23, 2014. https://www.crosswalk.com/blogs/christian-trends/10-signs-of-an-abusive-church.html)

trust what God says because they have been abused, ridiculed, neglected, and mistreated by the very people who were supposed to know better.

People who carried their Bibles all the time, knew Bible verses, had a good show of face. I have to remind you that the roach knows the Bible too and he uses many of "God's people" to carry out his dirty work.

If you have been hurt by a spiritual leader, or any believer, for that matter, take solace and thank God that He sees all and promises to separate the wheat from the tares. Like the parable of the farmer who said, "Let the weeds grow with the wheat, lest you pull up the wheat with them." Even those who hurt you have their purposes for a season. Forgive them and move on. God knows what He's doing.

I know it sucks, but God is the only one who truly knows how to love us well, and He loves us past our pain. I urge you not to throw the baby out with the bath water. God is still good, and just like Jesus said when referring to the religious leaders of His day: "So practice and obey whatever they tell you, but don't follow their example. For they don't practice what they teach." (Mt. 23:3,NLT)

They served their purpose in your life even if it was seasonal. God has seen everything you went through and cares for you. He is true love. He is the one who defines it, not the media, not emotion, not feelings, not your parents, not even your pastor; God is love. He is the only one who knows how to love you well, even when it doesn't fit your idea of love.

When We're the Problem

I'm going to keep this portion short and sweet. **Hurt people hurt people**. Up until now, I focused on people who have harmed us, but what happens when we are the problem? What happens when we fail to represent God in the way He intended for us to represent Him? I have been guilty of this on many occasions.

It's easy for us to focus on what others have done to us and excuse our own behavior, even as Christians. A lot of the trauma we have experienced has formed who we are and most likely has tainted our walk. We are innately evil and so we must be trained in how not to be that way.

Yes, we were hurt, but that does not excuse our own behavior and how God wants us to represent Him. Ultimately, no true change can happen without acknowledging what God did for us through Jesus on the cross.

Firstly, God loves you. When you realize you have hurt someone, ask Him for forgiveness and forgive yourself. Then, if possible, apologize to the people you have hurt and reconcile with them. Understand that even if they have not forgiven you, you are squared away with the Almighty.

The Story of Sunshyne

I f there's one thing you need to know about me, it's that
I love animals. I have four dogs of my own. So it stands
to reason that God uses the things I love to minister to me.

Pictured above is who I like to call my firstborn fur baby.
I have had many childhood dogs, but Sunshyne is the first
dog I was entirely responsible for as a teenager. He has
seen me through a lot. Right after high school, I went to a
puppy store, found him, and couldn't let him go. I had always
had big dogs growing up, but I was in my Paris Hilton phase

and wanted to carry a little dog around all the time. Oh, brother. Let's say he's been with me from B.C. to A.D. (if you know what I mean). He even predates my relationship with my husband, which says a lot since we were high school sweethearts. At the time this book is written, Sunshyne is a happy, fourteen-year old boy.

Being the O.G. of the house and with me by himself for a long time, he knows me. He knows everything about me, my character, and my love for him. Many things have changed since I got him from that puppy store so long ago. I've lost family members, got a boyfriend, married said boyfriend, found Jesus, lost friends because of Jesus, had a baby, and he was there for every sad moment to lick my tears away, and wagging his tail for every joyous one.

One morning, I had forgotten to fill up the dogs' water bowl. I don't know what happened that day, but it completely slipped my mind. While in the hustle and bustle of the day, trying to get some things done around the house, I walked into the kitchen and saw Sunshyne just sitting in front of the water bowl, paws crossed, and patiently waiting for me to come in to see him and fill it up. I don't think you got that. The little dog knew I loved him and trusted that eventually I would pass by him, see his need, and fulfill it.

My mind was blown.

And I was convicted. I have three other dogs who were probably also just as thirsty but didn't decide to let the person who could solve their problem know they were in need.

I identified with the other three dogs, and it shook me.

How many of us are willing to wait on God like that? How many of us will do everything in our power except pray for something so simple? He wants such a relationship with us that whenever we need something, we can come to Him and know that He is a loving Father. How much more does God love us? Little Sunshyne knew I loved him, and knew when I passed by I would recognize that he was thirsty. He knew I would never let him die of thirst, and in his own gentle way, reminded me of his need.

Now there's a dog who knows how to pray.

I don't know God's set up with the animal kingdom, but I'm convinced they pray. The Word does say to let everything that has breath praise, so why can't they pray too? When Sunshyne was younger, all he had to do was look at me, and my food would fall off my plate. It was like clockwork, and I was astonished. I mean, I didn't much care for it at the time when my whole drumstick would hit the floor, but talk about the power of petty prayer.

There's a worship song I love called "Fill me up" by Tasha Cobbs Leonard [4], which reminds me of our constant need for the infilling of the Holy Spirit. How many of us sing that song or pray for God to fill us up, and yet don't empty ourselves to be filled with God's love and for Him to fulfill our every need. We must choose to accept His love because He is the originator. There is no filter, no water bowl that is too big or small for Him to fill. All we have to do is ask. The Bible says to cast all your cares on him, and I mean all. Don't let a little dog out-pray you!! "…are you not more valuable than they" (Mt. 6:26).

---

[4] Cobbs Leonard, Tasha. "Fill me Up. Motown Gospel. Accessed December 1, 2021. https://music.apple.com/us/album/fill-me-up-live/1445017628?i=1445017996)

The Hard Part: When God feels silent

When you start to move in your purpose and get close to God, the roach gets angry. Of course, he does. he's a hater remember, and he wants you in misery with him. he doesn't like that you've stopped eating from the forbidden fruit and he's lost another person he can torture for eternity: another person he can use to hurt God's heart.

That pest has tried any and everything to get me to stop believing and walking with God. I have had an auto-immune disease, attacks on my emotions and marriage, stupid sinus headaches, a plague of annoying people, being misunderstood by others and outright being lied about and rejected. All this took a toll on me until my God asked me, "Are you better than your master?" (Jn. 15:20)

That question broke me.

My heart was straight up humbled. He dealt with all these things and more, and He was sinless. He endured all this for our sakes, for our dirt, for our transgressions. Given the roach does not have authority over us, God at times will use those very tactics to teach His children a lesson and let us stand apart in the midst of the chaos with joy and peace. I mean, everyone is going through it right now, but God's people stand out in hope and in power.

In all my trials, God has brought me out on the other side, stronger, better, faster, deeper in prayer and closer to Him. He has made me realize that feelings are just that, feelings. His truth is what matters. If He feels silent, we must remember that the teacher is always silent during the test.

Now this part isn't for everyone. Not everyone will go straight into war with the roach and his roach-ettes. But I need to let you know that war is upon us whether we acknowledge it or not. Think about it: in a physical war, can we choose to ignore the tanks and grenades going off around us while we walk to the grocery store? Will our heads not be always on a swivel? That's how silly it is not to acknowledge our spiritual war. If our nation is at war, we are at war. We were born into a war, an open war, and our only option is to choose a side.

I don't know about you, but I like to win. So if God has already won, that's the side I'm trying to be on.

God Wants to be Involved

Maybe someone hurt you, belittled you. Maybe someone didn't take your feelings into consideration, maybe you were abused by someone who was supposed to know God. Maybe being on this Earth with not-so-good people makes you have trust issues and not really believe you can ever be loved in the way you deserve. Heck, maybe something deeply terrible happened to you and you wonder how God could ever let you go through that type of pain. Trust me when I say that God can and does love you past your pain, despite your faults, and just because, with no strings attached. He cried with you during all the hurt and the pain. He is ready and able not only to forgive but to heal the hurt that pains you and use that very pain to build you and propel you into who you were meant to be. The Holy Spirit is a gift that is readily available to us. All we have to do is ask. God knows how to give good gifts. (Mt. 7:11)

COFFEE BREAK

Guess what? Time for another coffee break!

FREEDOM IN CHRIST

In June of 2015, I was diagnosed with Multiple Sclerosis (MS). I thought my life was over. I had to quit my amazing job, stress over always being in the ER, and struggle with the guilt of feeling like a burden to my loved ones. I was so depressed and disappointed in God because I thought, "If I'm Your daughter, why would You let this happen to me?"

I asked Him several times to heal me. Now when I say several times, I mean like a million. It was the first thing I thought about when I woke up and the last thing on my mind before bed. When I wasn't healed, I was even more disappointed.

I felt enslaved by my condition because my body was doing things I didn't want it to do. I was forced to alter my lifestyle and change how my life functioned because of this illness. I was in pain, lonely, and felt useless because I couldn't work.

I was in pure grief over the loss of my physical freedom, but most of all, from God's silence. Have you ever been in a situation where you believe God is working, but it's hard to see because you're clouded by your circumstance? That's where I was.

But God!

One day out of the blue, I remember sulking about my situation, wondering if God even heard my cries, and I heard Him ask me:

"Am I good?"

I said, "Yes."

"Do you believe I love you?"

I said, "Yes."

Then He asked me, "Am I still good if I don't heal you?"

That question broke me.

It made me realize that I had been questioning God's goodness and His love for me based on His response to my request. I had made Him a good and loving God based on His answer to my prayers.

I had to take a step back and ask myself: What is He teaching me through this illness?

What am I learning right now?

I can't say that I know everything He's teaching me because I still struggle. However, I know He has taught me that I am not in control and I need to let go and let Him lead me. I was the queen of planning and making sure things went according to plan, whether it be education, job, marriage, etc. I was like the family secretary and, in many ways, still am. Let's just say MS wasn't part of my five-year plan.

But it was part of His...

My body may be in bondage, but my spirit is free. Honestly, it took being in bondage even to understand what freedom meant. It wasn't until I let go that it dawned on me that sometimes God has to let you be in captivity to truly set you free. And you know what? I wouldn't trade my newfound liberty for a cure, because freedom in Christ is unparalleled.

My loneliness has given me alone time with God. Not working has given me time to work on my writing and to do His work. Understanding that I'm not in control has given me the freedom to give my burdens to God and to just be a kid, protected by her Father's love. My pain has given me the gift of relating to people in sorrow and encouraging those like me in the truth that God has not forgotten them.

I'm no longer in the shackles of defeat, for by His stripes, we are healed. Sometimes, the healing you wanted isn't the one you truly needed. Although I still pray for physical healing, I am content knowing and trusting that it is on His time. And may His will be done, not mine.

Now, friend, there will be times that you struggle with thoughts of defeat, and circumstances may seem impossible to overcome. But if you keep your eyes on God, step back and look at the whole picture, you will see that God is working miracles through your plight, and He is faithful to carry you through.

Remember that God has a reason for everything He's doing in your life. He uses all your experiences, the good, the bad, and even the ugly, to mold you into the person you were designed to be. Your pain and response to it may even be helping others. So, believe that God is good and He loves you despite the rain, and remember that April showers make flowers bloom in May.

Sometimes it takes a painful situation to make us change our ways. (Pr. 20:30)

Questions:

1. Where has God felt silent in your life?

2. Have you prayed about it or are you in a place of defeat?
3. Is God still good to you if He doesn't fix it?

A Not-so-Brief Interruption

T he day I finished the first draft of this book, on my birthday this year, a dear friend of mine committed suicide. In my spirit I felt something was off that day, but couldn't quite put my finger on it. Everything in my body hurt, I was clouded, couldn't think straight, but I had made a deal with the Lord that the first draft would be finished on my birthday, and with a lot of battles, it was finished.

The next morning, my husband got the call. I was confused and knowing it was something bad because my husband sat down and started to tear up. There's one thing I have to let you know about Tony: he doesn't cry. Like not really. I can count on one hand how many times I've seen him cry and it has to be something really, really bad. He put the phone down and told me and I immediately let out this screeching cry.

A little backstory on me, I have lost a lot of people in my short life (see Miracle Dog story later in this book). I do not cry immediately. I usually am in some sort of denial before it truly hits me.

This hit me immediately. I knew my friend struggled with some things, and in all honesty was not surprised. I was angry. Angry that the roach would convince my friend to take his own life. Angry at the state of Christianity today, where someone can be very evidently dealing with demonic oppression and not get the help that we are commanded to give because the roach has conditioned us to be so complacent and afraid.

However, even in this, the roach did not win. My friend was a believer. He tried his hardest with the tools he was given, and ultimately, the good Lord allowed him to go this way. I take solace in the fact that the only prerequisite to ending up in heaven is that you believe and follow Christ to the best of your ability. He was loved by many and will be extremely missed. I thank God that He is using even this tragedy to open the eyes of those whom the roach has blinded. In this, my friend's death was not in vain, and I can be happy that he is resting in the arms of his Father.

No matter what we have gone through, who has hurt us, or even if God feels silent, He is always with us. Even if Jesus is asleep on the boat in the middle of your storm, like He was with the disciples, know that He's got this. If Jesus has promised that you would get to the other side, and He's asleep, this means He is un-bothered and we need to learn to also be un-bothered and have faith in His plan.

I know trusting Him with all these layers of insecurity is easier said than done, especially since some situations on this Earth can be straight up trifling, but know that He wants you to "bother" Him, and even to be annoying if you have to be. Unlike humans, He appreciates the constant dependence for every single detail. (Lk. 18:1-8)

Our feelings are valid to God and He cares for them all, but we mustn't let emotion be the driving factor in our lives, especially since the roach knows he can toy with them, using all the things mentioned in the previous chapter and more.

Love and trust are a choice, and if we choose to trust God, He promises to save us from all of the enemy's scare tactics. If you gotta scream, **"God cares about me,"** out loud to drown out all the noise, do it. If you have to openly talk to God in public like I do, do it. It may seem a little crazy, but there are plenty of things that people thought Jesus was crazy for doing and saying, and I guess we just have to look crazy like our God.

God uses all of life's troubles, all our history, and even lets the roach hit us a little just to create the perfect scenario and discipline so we are ready for when He brings us hope and a future. (Jer. 29:11)

Oh, that must feel like crap to the roach. All that hard work trying to destroy our lives, just for us to still come out on top. **Ouch.**

I love my Petty Petty God.

Let's Get Petty

A lifestyle of petty prayer

"A Lion does not turn around when a dog barks"~
African Proverb

Now that we know God cares about every single detail, how do we start taking active steps in praying purposefully petty prayers that shake the heavens and bring down manna?

Answer: Pray for a good hair day....

And rebuke the roach's attempts at disturbing your cuteness.

It's really that simple, but between our never-friendly neighborhood pest combined with our own pride and trust issues, we tend to fight praying for something that small.

Growing up, the only time I went to God was for the big things, which was rare, especially since I had a pretty cushy childhood. I can say that as a child, I prayed about only the things I did wrong during confession time at my then Catholic church, or I prayed when Easter rolled around, and on Christmas to the nativity scene, or honestly to that Mary statue so we could pose for pictures. In reality, I had no big things to pray about, so praying was few and far between until God allowed me to get some real-life experiences. Those experiences would shock my system into realizing that this cushy life I had could come to a screeching halt at any given moment. In fact, it did, in every single way.

Let's take another Coffee Break, shall we?

COFFEE BREAK: Miracle Dog (My Come to Christ testimony)

"I was at a breaking point. It would literally take one more event to send me over the edge."

Now I should say semi-testimony. There are so many things that have led me to God, but I felt this story was an amazing one. It's also the event that made me realize this God I was searching for was a powerful one.

God uses the things you love to teach you lessons and surprise! (not a surprise) it involves a little dog named Dahab.

Let's start from the beginning...

Without saying too much, before I found God, I was in a terrible place. If you have ever heard that saying "when it rains it pours," at this point in my life that saying was my autobiography. Starting around the time I was fifteen going on sixteen, everything started going wrong. At fifteen, I lost my maternal grandmother, whom I was extremely close to. I didn't know it then, but her death would be the start to a series of events that would crush my otherwise seemly perfect little existence into pieces. Now, my grandmother was a devout Christian who lived her life in love and peace. Her legacy is that she was the spiritual backbone of our family. I know you're saying, "Everyone loses their grandma, this is unfortunate but it's a part of life."

But wait, there's more...

I was in high school at the time, already dealing with the drama of being a teenager plus some additionally stressful high school drama. I won't go into details for the sake of time, but let's just say I met my future husband in high school, but I was a teenager, stupid and emotional. At the same time, my mother blacked out while driving and got into a car accident. We found out that she suffered from a brain aneurysm. She survived but she was away from us for a year and a half.

My dad, although he worked full time, didn't know how to handle the finances, as this was something my mother took care of. I decided I had to grow up fast. I learned what a mortgage was, how to pay bills, how to cook, how to clean, and I also had to get my schoolwork done with a lot of extra credit, because my brother and I were out of school for two months after the accident. I wanted to graduate on time, so I worked really hard that year.

I was thrown into adulthood at seventeen years old. While I was mature for my age, I was still very much a child who was going through high school drama, without her mom, in a year that she would go to prom, graduate high school and turn eighteen years old.

Within a year, I lost my adopted grandfather/family friend, my paternal grandmother *(she was extremely sick with cancer and also lived with me)*, and my aunt *(she died two weeks after my mom's accident)*. My cat was poisoned by accident *(he died the same night my aunt died)*, and my uncle *(my mom's brother and the one who lost his wife)* had to get his leg amputated due to complications from diabetes. Now, I was really close to my uncle, so it hurt deeply to see a father figure of mine so weak.

Think that's it? Nope!

I went to prom with my future husband (then dating/confused) but was still in this high school drama situation. I ended up staying home on graduation day because I didn't want to go to a ceremony that my mom wasn't a part of. Honestly, the only reason I went to prom was that Tony asked me and he wouldn't take no for an answer. I thank him for that because I would have missed two milestones.

By this point, I had turned eighteen without my mom and had to go to prom without her fixing my hair and telling me I looked beautiful. I didn't have a long line of family members taking pictures, which was what I had always expected. I had one friend there to take pictures and I thank him for capturing the memory for us, because we wouldn't have any memories at all. Prom was fun, but graduation was not for me. Not without my mom. I took a year off from college and took a part-time job in an effort to help my dad pay the bills.

The next year, a few weeks before my nineteenth birthday, my mom came home! We were all super thankful that she survived and could once again be with us. I started college, I had entered a committed relationship with my future husband, and all was seemingly getting back to normal.

But not for me…

You see, I had been in a state of autopilot and survival mode for years before this. I never had a chance to process all the things that were happening to me. I was deeply depressed but hadn't come to terms with it yet.

Then, just when I thought I had time to process all the events that had happened, my uncle *(the one who had his leg amputated)* got into a car accident.

That same day, my dog Max died. The day of my uncle's accident, Max had been really sick and my uncle was supposed to drive us to the vet. Max died twenty minutes before we got the phone call from the hospital. My uncle was unscathed by the accident, but the car was totaled.

We thought we had escaped the worst, but a week later, my uncle fell down his front porch and broke both his arms. He spent hours on the porch, yelling for help, before someone passing by saw him and called an ambulance. Picture this: he only had one working leg, and both his arms were broken.

He was in the hospital for three weeks. My mom was with him every single day. The day that the whole family went to visit him, my part-time job wouldn't let me have the day off, but I thought, "No big deal, I'll just go by myself during the week…"

He died that very night of a heart attack.

My mom told me he asked for me. Of course, he did. I was his goddaughter. He claimed godfather rights over me at my birth. I was his favorite and only niece. He and my father were both supposed to walk me down the aisle when I got married. But instead, he died before he could do any of that.

His death caused an all-time low for me.

At this point, I was tired of life. I wouldn't say I was suicidal, but I thought death had to be better than this. I lost another one of my childhood dogs to old age within months of my uncle's death. Honestly, the only thing that kept me from thinking suicidal thoughts was that I knew the impact it would have on my family if I died. But still, my mind was constantly on death.

My husband (then boyfriend) knew I wasn't okay. He had been around for pretty much all these events, with the exception of my maternal grandmother. A few months before my mom came home, I had gotten my precious baby Sunshyne. He was there to lick all the tears off my face and cheer me up. I wanted another chihuahua to keep him company, and also because there's no better pick-me-up than a fur baby. I found this little guy up for adoption online and instantly fell in love.

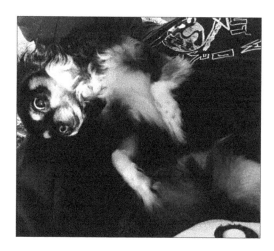

His owner couldn't keep him because she had just had a baby and was moving back to Egypt. As a gift, Tony paid the adoption fee. We went to pick him up and Dahab was ours. It's pretty amazing how quickly a pet can become part of your family. Everyone loved him, just look at that face.

The Miracle

Around this time, I had started to seek God. I wasn't sure why I was pulled to faith, but I would come to find out that all these events were allowed to happen so He could bring me to Him.

Sometimes God has to get rid of the idols in His place so He can take His rightful position in your heart. My husband asked me a few years ago why I decided to go to God after all of the events that transpired in my life. I replied, "Because I had nothing else."

My family was an idol. I had the family you saw in the movies. The movies weren't even a fantasy for me, I lived it in real life. I had a multi-racial family with two parents who loved each other, brothers who protected me at all costs, a house with pets, living grandparents, and even my extended family was close. But I didn't know God. I knew of Him, but He was just the guy we talked to in our Thanksgiving prayers and the reason we got gifts on Christmas. I was empty and vain.

However, at this point in my life, my picture-perfect situation had gotten several large doses of reality.

I was still very much depressed, but I was going to Bible study and getting counseling at my college. I was at a breaking point. It would literally take one more event to send me over the edge.

Then that event happened…

I was walking home from Bible study one night and started down my street when I saw Dahab crawl under our chain link fence and run out into the road. A car was coming down the block. I screamed. The car hit and ran over him. I heard him squeal as the car crushed his body. The car stopped as I ran down the block in utter shock, assuming that I would be scraping his body off the pavement.

At that moment, I said, "God, You know where I am right now mentally. **This is it for me."**

While I ran toward the scene, I saw Dahab crawl out from underneath the car. His back legs were completely crushed and he was walking toward me with his two front paws. I slowed down a little bit because I couldn't believe what I was seeing…

Right in front of my eyes, as he was walking my way, his back legs started to heal and he started running toward me. **I was in disbelief.**

I grabbed him, not believing what I had just witnessed, and picked him up. I started bawling uncontrollably. I took him to my porch and continued crying. I had been saving money from my part-time job and I decided to use that and take him to the vet to get checked out. I called my husband (boyfriend at the time) to pick me up. I told him what happened and I don't know if he thought I was crazy or if he knew what to make of what I was saying. All he knew was that I was a blubbering mess.

He lived a few minutes away, so he came right over and we rush to the emergency vet. They took Dahab's x-rays and saw nothing wrong with him. The people at the hospital didn't even believe what I was saying. They didn't believe that he was really run over by a car. But as a mark of this miracle, he had a tiny scratch on his stomach and to this day has a dip in the shape of a tire in his back, even though the x-ray didn't show any breaks and he is still a perfectly healthy dog (beyond healthy even). They couldn't even explain the dip in the ER.

I'm feeling the urge to just break out into worship right now. LOL

God saw where I was and saved that little dog for me. He knew I was at my breaking point. If I didn't live it and see it with my own two eyes, I wouldn't have believed it.

In that one event, He showed me His power, His love, and His mercy all at the same time. He made it undeniably evident that He is real! Dahab was one year old at the time of the accident. He is now a happy, active thirteen-year-old boy.

God taught me that He sees and takes care of those who seek Him. He made me understand that even though I was going through trials and didn't know Him, He was always with me. He has given me a story of surrender and of victory all at the same time.

From that day on...

I knew not only that God was real, but that He was really *For Me*.

Questions:

1. Have you ever experienced a miracle? If so, how did it change your life?
2. How has God been faithful in your lowest moments?

I wish I could say following this giant miracle that I immediately went into trusting God fully, but that is far from the truth. It would be years before I developed that kind of relationship with God, and I still struggle at times. There was still so much healing that needed to take place. All I knew was that in my darkest moment, God saved a little dog for me, with whom most people would feel like I didn't have enough history to love yet, but you know what? I received my petty miracle with joy.

I'm here to tell you that you don't have to take as long as I did. Even if it has been years or decades, as long as there is breath in your lungs, you can start to trust God with your every need. You are never too old, or too young.

Once I developed a relationship with God, there were still a lot of things that I would think were way too small to bring to Him. There were many seemingly small situations that I thought I should definitely be able to handle myself, which would have gone way differently had I trusted in God. In fact, those very small things led to some really big problems. And because I wasn't seeking God daily to help me change my behavior, I was stuck in a never-ending cycle that would ultimately need the hand of God.

During the time of my mother's accident, it never dawned on me to pray for the small stuff, nor did I even really know what or how to pray. I was so focused on this giant tragedy that praying for everyday life felt insignificant.

Yes, God allowed all these events to shock me into salvation, but it took a long time for me to believe that God would do anything for our situation. It took a really long time to even understand that God wanted to help me and that I should even seek Him. I went on autopilot, trying to figure out everything on my own, trying to step up and dance to the "act like an adult" theme song to my life. All the while, I was suffering emotionally and spiritually.

On the grander scale of things, my spiritual and emotional state compared to all the death and tragedy I had experienced felt meaningless, but even so, I couldn't shake how I felt.

God, in His own way, was using the big things to lead me to pray about the seemingly petty things, which would lead into having faith that can move mountains.

Yup… that was a mouthful. Let me explain. God doesn't always go in order. Not our order, anyway, and the mysteries of God wouldn't be mysteries if we understood it all. In essence, God wouldn't be God if we could always figure out what He's up to. However, I'm going to try to explain what I mean when I say that He basically brought me on a loop.

When my mother had her accident, that was a big thing. I didn't know what else to do but take action myself. I did everything that I could do to be a "big girl" and step up and do what I had to do for our family. In and of itself, that was not a bad thing to do, however, it was missing a key component. God.

I felt burdened to basically take my mother's place. There was a lot of pressure in trying to get everything done, going to see my mother, figuring out how to pay bills, manage a household, learn how to cook, all so I could try to help keep my family afloat. So many people died, and I still didn't pray like I should. I was just doing. Going and going like the Energizer Bunny, except I'm not a battery. And neither are you. I had practiced doing for myself so much that it became an idol. I mean, it always was, but now it was about survival. I was a slave to the pressures of life.

The Rat Race

A lot of people are stuck in the rat race in life, and I have been no different. We get into this daily grind of going to work, coming home, eating, and doing it all over again the next day. We say a quick prayer, go to church on Sunday, go home and come Monday morning, we're back at it again. Wash, rinse and repeat.

Christians are not immune to this vicious cycle. So many of us feel like we need to do more, be more, serve more, and have everything together, when salvation is a free gift. This mindset as believers can be detrimental to the faith and to our families. Many children leave the faith altogether when they are older because their parents didn't give them the attention and care they were commanded to give them in training them up, because their parents felt like training them in the faith was about following a bunch of rules. The same is true of spiritual fathers as well. We have in essence become slaves to laws we have created, just like the pharisees. We must pray that we can come to the full knowledge of how much Jesus has set us free.

The cycles in our lives are extremely hard to break, especially since in the eyes of the world, we are doing what we are supposed to do.

For me, I did everything I felt I needed to do in my own strength to survive, to help my family survive and strive just to make a little more money here and there. Before I knew it, I was stuck on a never-ending hamster wheel. Always running but staying in the same place. Stagnant. We never believe there is better for ourselves, especially since this is something usually passed down for generations, like it was for me. How many of our parents, uncles, aunts, grandparents, etc., stayed at a job they hated for forty-five years? It may look different for you and me, and we may justify it by doing things that are not in themselves wrong, but ultimately, we tend to repeat the same habits of our forefathers.

I was taught not to depend on anyone but myself. In a worldly view, there is nothing wrong with that, until we recognize that we have been treating God like that untrustworthy friend or family member. When my mother had her accident, we found out really quickly who our real friends were and who were basically wolves in sheep's clothing.

That time period in my life was a lot of self-discovery, and I am sure you have gone through similar periods of life where God is letting you go through the fire to refine you. The end result is that we are forged into iron, but if we're being honest, it's never fun. I mean… it's fire, its hot and it burns.

If we're being real, the rat race is a comfortable place to be. But there is no progress. No real life or spiritual breakthrough. Going to church, reading your Bible, evangelizing, work, school, marriage, children, and everything that is in your day-to-day becomes formulaic, and basically another thing that is checked off on your to-do list during the week.

God doesn't want to be a checklist item. He wants a relationship. He wants to be personally involved in every single thing for your good and for His glory. He is your Creator and created you for a relationship with Him and others. He is the Almighty God, and we are constantly out here acting like

He's some sort of basic God. We need to put some respect on His name and His love.

I remember a time where I was so overwhelmed spiritually. It was like spiritual overload. Like I was hearing God's voice and direction on everything. (I still do, but I'm used to it now.) He was talking to me about everything, down to the way I wore my hair or something minor like that.

In my ignorance, I asked: "God, can I do anything without You?"

He replied: "You can't even wake up without Me."

Y'all, I was shaken. He was right. My very breath was a product of His mercy. It's funny how we move through life, every single day, expecting to wake up, expecting to get to work safely, expecting to get to school, expecting a meal, expecting all these things, when all these things are gifts. Gifts that we take for granted every single day. Every single breath we take is an act of mercy. Now, I'm not saying to pray after every breath, but it would be nice if you gave the gift giver some credit for His handiwork daily.

Like for real, the fact that you can see, hear, taste, smell, and touch things is a gift. Even if you can't do some of these things, the others are a blessing. There are so many things we take for granted in this world. Candidly, I believe that's why the good Lord allowed the pandemic. It has brought so many things into perspective for so many different people. Parents started to realize that they are missing out on their kids' lives, people are realizing that they missed time with their family, heck, people are even adopting more pets because of the pandemic.

Long story not so short: after all those catastrophic things happened to my family, I thought it couldn't be any worse than this. God saved my little dog (petty thing). That event would take me on a journey of discovery about how much God really cares about details and justice. The enemy knew that taking that little dog would break me, but God saw it as an opportunity to show His mercy, even though I didn't really seek Him during the big stuff. He used the deaths and accidents as a way to make me realize all these things could come to a crashing halt, but when God saved Dahab, my faith grew even bigger as God proved His faithfulness.

THE RESET

As a result of our conditioning, we really need to change the way we think in regard to our relationship with God and what we go to Him for. By ourselves, we just can't change, because it's what we know and we have adapted to this mindset so much that it's part of who we are. We were basically born this way. Think about it: trying to do it for ourselves started in the garden. This is so generational that it's from the beginning of time!

As I said, I was taught not to depend on anyone for anything. It took a while, but I came to realize that God allowing MS was His grace. I'm hardheaded, and I really actually enjoy doing things myself and not depending on people. Don't we all? So, what better way for God to cause a glitch in my programming than to put me in a situation where I have to depend on people physically?

In His mercy, He has not allowed me to be immobilized, but I have limitations that alter the way I have to live my life. And what better way to learn how to pray daily and to pray pettily than when you have to ask God for strength to walk properly today? It kept me in constant communication with Him, which strengthened my connection to Him.

He taught me through this illness that we all should be praying that way, even if we have no physical issues, because literally every part of our lives is mercy.

In the following chapters, I will outline what has worked for me to establish the father and daughter relationship that I have with God, and prayerfully, you will also come to the knowledge that your God is intimately involved in every aspect of your life.

Decide

Prerequisite

"But as for me and my house we will serve the Lord"~
Joshua 24:15

Decide to serve the Lord. You can run through the following steps, but ultimately, God wants to build a relationship with you. We can't add these steps as checks on a to-do list like we have been doing in every other aspect of our lives. It needs to be an intentional step toward getting to know our Lord.

He wants you to want to get to know Him or at least have made a decision to follow Him and/or to try to figure out who He is. Heck, I even recommend this to unbelievers who are seeking. They'll be so surprised when Jesus greets them at the door.

Otherwise, this is just motivational speaking and not an active act of pursuit. He will pick up the slack wherever we fall short. However, if we have our minds made up, it is easier for God to move through us and for us. Don't get me wrong, God in all His sovereignty can always make a way, and has factored in our stupidity, but our minds being made

GOD HEARS YOUR PETTY PRAYERS

up is the difference between a straight path and taking the scenic route.

Some might not think taking the scenic route is all that bad, but think about it being like a traffic jam and every time you move, there's an accident in the way. If we have not made up our minds that we will see this thing through, it will be an uphill battle as we will constantly be in confusion.

Decide that no matter what, you will see this thing to the end no matter how much it takes, even if the roach has convinced you it's pointless. Commit to what you believe God is saying and He will see you through it.

Although this is not a task list, it is important not only to set goals but to make plans to succeed in them. I have to be real with you, taking these steps is an act of war against the roach. It is the best strategy to prepare for attacks before they even arise. The Lord is your ultimate protector, and He will see you through to the end. However, because as humans we are already prone to double-mindedness and to making excuses for ourselves, the enemy tries to come in and snatch away that motivation immediately to keep us stagnant in our faith, never evolving into greater heights with God, comfortable.

This part is important because le roach will throw all kinds of things at you to try to get you to stop once you start. he will cause you to slip up even when you have a plan. So not having a plan is like fighting with one hand tied behind your back. I mean, we're made in His image, right? Didn't God have a plan when He created the Earth?

Fasting

Step 1

"Return to me with all your heart with fasting"~ Joel 2:12

Fasting is how all this started for me. There is nothing that brings you closer to God than giving up something that sustains your body for what sustains your soul. (Jn. 4:13-14) Fasting brings into perspective how fragile our lives are and how much we take for granted. God uses these moments when we deprive our bodies to bring us closer to Him, spiritually. The Bible is full of examples of God's people fasting and receiving divine intervention. Jesus Himself said, "When you fast" (Mt. 6:16) versus "if" you fast. Which means He fully expects fasting to be a part of our lives. The prophets fasted, He fasted, why shouldn't we?

In this chapter, I'll start off by telling you some of my history with fasting, but also give you key tools and scripture to be successful in your fasts.

DISCLAIMER
Always check with your doctor before fasting especially if you have any underlying conditions. Also seek the Lord first.

I am telling you what worked for me and the miracles that God has done through this sacred act of dependence.

My First Group Fast

I'm not going to lie to you, in the beginning It was hard. Y'all, I love food, I love everything about it. The Good Lord has been gracious to me and decided to give me just enough control and a fast metabolism that I'm not 9,000 pounds, and the abuse of this gift was real. Everyone knew about it down to people I didn't even know that well at my former church. I mean, my love for food wasn't a very well-kept secret. I was at every function, eating with "no consequences." They had decided to fast, wanted to invite me, but knew I had a "problem," so to speak. They didn't think I would do it, but y'all, the FOMO (fear of missing out) was real. I just had to try this fast thing. But it was a juice fast. Wait... what? I mean the good Lord had been preparing my gluttonous self to fast, as I had done fruit and vegetable fasts before, but y'all, no chewing was hard. But my mind was made up. I had to.

The Lord orchestrated it so that we were all from different sections of the church. Most of us never really hung out. Outside of my best friend, we were all just getting to know each other through this initial fast. We were just Christian women who wanted to get closer to God and hopefully get some prayers and questions answered. Honestly, I had no idea what I was fasting for at the time, but God in all His sovereignty just wanted me to take a leap of faith and discover that He could move mountains for me.

By Day 3, I was ready to give up, but because my mind was made up and I had others doing the fast with me, I was empowered to keep pushing. After that three-day hump, it got easier. And it became like a diet, but boy did I just want a burger or something. The sucky thing was that at the end of the fast when I got said "burger" in the form of some chicken wings, I was so disappointed that the fast had changed my pallet. Thank God it was temporary. No one told me that would happen, so I looked at the chicken on my plate and pouted like an angry child who didn't get her ice cream.

During the fast, I had written an article and thought I was finished with it. On the second to last day of the fast, I woke up to the words "Behind You." It was five in the morning. At this point, I had no children and 5 am was an ungodly hour. I mean, it still feels like it is, but apparently the Good Lord likes that time, so what are you gonna do?

I was honestly trying to figure out if that was God or the other guy. The Lord says to test the spirit and that 5 am spirit didn't feel right. Also, I love to sleep, so that may have clouded my judgement. I looked behind me to see my husband peacefully sleeping and doing exactly what I wanted to be doing at 5 am on a Saturday.

I really wanted to go back to sleep, but I was stirred. I couldn't sleep. I picked up my phone as millennials tend to do, and decided to look at my article. At that moment, God started reminding me of things I had forgotten to include. I cried while writing it and it ended up being one of my most successful articles. Even more than that, I found out my husband not only decided to fast with me the remaining days of the fast, but was behind the scenes promoting my article. God showed me how much I needed his support. It was an unexpected blessing.

That article was "Freedom in Christ."

That impromptu fast, with women I barely knew, started a wave of events and a closeness with God that I never thought was possible. During this fast, I didn't even really know what I was fasting for, but God showed me a glimpse into what He had planned for my life.

So many petty miracles came out of that fast. While I was on the phone with a fellow faster, her mother, who suffered from mental illness and had long bouts of not speaking, spoke for the first time in a long time. People had breakthroughs in mindsets, work, and so much more. Something about denying yourself and cleansing your mind brings you into a space with God that really shows you from where your provision really comes.

If God had not provided the resources for even something as simple as eating, we would not survive. Fasting reminds me that this is a body I borrow and its every cell is subject to the Word of God. I recognize fasting is not something that a lot of people like to do, honestly, myself included at first, but once I got into fasting, I couldn't stop. I now have a scheduled fast weekly because God's hand is so supernaturally connected to fasting that I cannot deny its power. So, I'll give up that burger for a time if it means getting closer to God. We became closer to God like never before. Little did we know that God had even more planned for the next fast.

My Fast Baby

Now this is the real meat and potatoes. In the summer of 2019, God led us to do another fast. We went to our standard restaurant that we always went to for after church hangouts and made a "Fast-Plan." Hear this? I felt the **need** for a fast! **Me!** The hungry hungry hippo.

The crazy thing about this fast was that a lot of our friends from church came to the same hangout spot. Some people who were at the table hadn't actually intended to fast, and ended up fasting with us! They had no idea that God was about to change our lives forever.

I believe God had us practice with our first fast. We had a lot of failures last time and decided to make a set of rules so we knew exactly what we were doing. Some people had altered fasts due to medical concerns, leading from the Holy Spirit, or just what they felt they could commit to at the time. Most of us were on the juice fast for the entire seven days, and others broke fast each day at 6pm. For me, some days God didn't let me eat at all, and yet God did not differentiate between us. Blessings flowed to and through all of us on that fast.

We knew exactly where we failed the last time, and made a plan to cut down on failure and to really see this thing through, despite the temptations that the stinkbug would throw at us.

We made a list of acceptable ingredients for the juice fast: fruits, vegetables, and nuts. We decided soups that had no solids and no meat, no added sugar, etc., were acceptable. For some reason, last time we only did fruit juices and straight forgot about vegetables. Like I said, it's important to make a plan, but we learned from our mistakes and God understood our ignorance.

We made a list of acceptable programming, time to pray, and phone calls. Y'all, we had it down pat and still failed at times. We deleted social media from our phones, the whole nine yards. This is why a plan is important. Like the last time, there were people we weren't in close relationship with, but most of us were already part of the last fast and knew what God could do if we sought Him in this way.

So many miraculous things happened during that fast. The first day, while I probably still had plantains from the "Fast-Plan" dinner in my stomach, I had a dream that told me my husband shouldn't go to work.

MY FIRST FAST MIRACLE

Sometimes, I ask Tony to stay home just because I want to cuddle, but he ends up going to work most of the time. That day, I went back to sleep after he said no, and I heard the word "insist." Insist is not a word I normally use, so I heeded the warning and insisted. He was already feeling under the weather, so I told him he needed to stay home anyway.

He heeded my warning and stayed home. I didn't know what the Lord was preventing at that time, but I knew he had to be home. The entire time, le roach was trying to make me feel crazy, but I'd rather be safe than sorry. I messaged the group chat that morning with my dream, as we used that chat as a way to document what God was doing.

Around 2 pm, I started to think about what to make for our fast, especially since Tony had decided to do the fast with me from the beginning this time. We sat on our bed, and as I looked up recipes, Tony went through his work emails.

I suddenly heard him shout, "I don't like you," in a somewhat playful manner. We kid around like that sometimes when someone turns out to be right about something that the other didn't agree with. But this felt different. I looked at him with confusion and asked, "What did I do?"

He said, "I just got a work email warning the staff that a helicopter crashed in Manhattan, two blocks away from my job." Get this: the helicopter crashed on top of his former employer's building, at around the exact time that he would be in that area for lunch.

Of course, I updated the ladies! Not only did we now document the act of faith and obedience, we documented God's sovereignty. That morning, I was perfectly content, just knowing God protected us from "something," but the Good Lord wanted me to know what my faith did.

I did some further research that day and found out that a similar crash happened back in 1996 in which a woman on the ground passed away from falling debris. God revealed in my spirit that the enemy had planned to do that to my husband. Oh nah, roach. God always wins.

The week carried on just like that with so many other supernatural occurrences. All in all, God was active and we still had food in our stomachs. God used my experience as the catalyst on the faith trip that God was bringing us all on. This was literally the first day, scratch that, the first morning! What more could happen, right? The answer is: a lot, a whole lot more.

People were getting divine favor in ways they didn't expect, and most of all, a lot of us were privileged to be a blessing to others. We told our testimonies at the end of the fast and got to witness to people in the entire restaurant about God's faithfulness.

The Ultimate Miracle

Before, during, and after this fast, God was sending people to randomly pray over me, specifically over my womb.

It was the weirdest thing. People out of nowhere were feeling led by the Spirit to pray and were having dreams about me. In the meantime, my body had been acting weird for months.

TMI alert. My monthly cycle comes regularly. Like, you can count on my cycle like an old girlfriend. She came on time, every month. I knew her and she knew me. I didn't always like her, but we had an understanding. Then suddenly, she started to act brand new. Apparently, she started hanging out with a new group of friends because I barely recognized her.

For two months, the Lord messed up a cycle that I had come to depend on. It came but it came often. My counts were completely off. My husband and I didn't use protection, so this was the way we knew my ovulation dates. This was part of the reason Tony and I were able to hold off on children for a while, but God was getting ready to reveal to me that the roach had been doing things not only against my womb, but also getting me to agree with it the entire time. I didn't even know there was a problem. But God did, and He was getting ready to make His mighty power known.

During the fast, while watching a Christian program and doing my hair at the same time (don't judge me), I accidentally got some hair product in my eyes. Y'all, my eyes were on fire. In a panic, I ran to the bathroom to get some Visine and screamed "Jesus!" I pressed as hard as I could to get the Visine out of the bottle. It wouldn't come out. I checked to see if the bottle was finished, if it was crusted over in any way. Heck, I looked to see if the cap was off and everything was fine. It just wouldn't come out. I then started to notice that my eye was feeling better. I just had to take a video because I needed proof that I wasn't crazy. I sent it to the girls in the fast chat and they were all amazed. But of course, here comes that spider, crawling up the water spout of doubt, into my ear.

By this point, the Lord was sending a lot of not-so-subtle messages that I was pregnant. My cycle was crazy late and I was convinced that I may have been, but in all honestly, my cycle was acting funky for the last two months but always eventually came. Sometimes, I thought she was just being temperamental, as is often evident in the level of cramping I used to get. But like I said, I would rather be safe than sorry. The Holy Spirit led me to throw out a bunch of my skin products, start eating right, and I even stopped drinking any alcohol. Y'all, God had me moving like I was pregnant before I was pregnant.

But I digress, back to the Visine bottle. I found it so weird that the Visine bottle wouldn't open and that my eye miraculously started to feel better. So, I looked up Visine and pregnancy and found out that it's not good for pregnant women. I searched the cracks of the Internet to find that article. The next day, I wondered, "Did the Lord really stop a bottle for me because I was pregnant?" I had to go check that bottle out. Maybe there was something wrong with it. I went into my bathroom, took the cap off the Visine, and Y'all, it flowed like Niagara Falls. Welp, Lord, thank You for protecting me. I was amazed at how God protected me from something even my friend who is an ER nurse didn't know.

All in all, I wasn't officially pregnant at that time, but you see, God was opening my mind to having a baby. I was so scared of the thought that I had been throwing arrows at my own womb. God used that time to purge me of speaking death into my womb and led those people to pray over my womb for protection against the enemy.

I got my period after the Visine miracle, and I felt sad. It was strange, since my cycle was something that I prayed for monthly. Why would I be sad? I'll tell you why.

I asked God, "Why are You putting me through this roller coaster of emotions?" I heard in my spirit, "So that My name would be glorified." And glorified it was.

That was my last period.

My pregnancy was counted from the day after our fast ended. I was already pregnant in God's eyes.

> *"He settles the childless woman in her home*
> *as a happy mother of children" (Ps. 113:9)*

HOW TO FAST

I'm not going to tell you how to fast, because that needs to be guided by the Holy Spirit, the Word of God, and your own dietary restrictions, but I am going to help you build a "Fast-Plan" that will help you to organize and thwart the enemies' plans to derail you. That pest is scared of fasts, and he will do anything he can to keep you from the knowledge of its true power.

Let's start with some scripture about fasting and temptation:

FASTING

> *So we fasted and petitioned our God about this,*
> *and he answered our prayer. (Ezra 8:23, NIV)*

> *Jesus, full of the Holy Spirit, left the Jordan*
> *and was led by the Spirit into the wilderness,*
> *where for forty days he was tempted by the*

devil. He ate nothing during those days, and at the end of them he was hungry. (Lk. 4:1-2, NIV)

"While they were worshiping the Lord and fasting, the Holy Spirit said, "Set apart for me Barnabas and Saul for the work to which I have called them. So after they had fasted and prayed, they placed their hands on them and sent them off." (Acts 13:1-3. NIV)

Moses was there with the Lord forty days and forty nights without eating bread or drinking water. And he wrote on the tablets the words of the covenant—the Ten Commandments. (Ex. 4:28, NIV)

I ate no choice food; no meat or wine touched my lips; and I used no lotions at all until the three weeks were over. (Dan. 10:3, NIV)

Is not this the kind of fasting I have chosen:
to loose the chains of injustice
and untie the cords of the yoke,
to set the oppressed free
and break every yoke? (Is. 58:6, NIV)

"Even now," declares the Lord,
"return to me with all your heart,
with fasting and weeping and mourning."
(Jo. 2:12, NIV)

Based on these Scriptures, we can see that not only is fasting expected of us, but that God views it as a way of acknowledging our dependence on Him. This allows us to stray away from the human tendency for self-sufficiency and in turn gets Him to draw us closer as His children. Furthermore, as we can see in Acts 13:1-3 and Ezra 8:23, fasting activates answers for our prayers as well as our ministries and callings.

Now let's look at what God says about temptation.

TEMPTATION

> No temptation has overtaken you except what is common to mankind. And God is faithful; he will not let you be tempted beyond what you can bear. But when you are tempted, he will also provide a way out so that you can endure it. (1 Cor. 10:13, NIV)

> Blessed is the one who perseveres under trial because, having stood the test, that person will receive the crown of life that the Lord has promised to those who love him. (Jms. 1:12, NIV)

> When tempted, no one should say, "God is tempting me." For God cannot be tempted by evil, nor does he tempt anyone. (Jms. 1:13, NIV)

> You know what I long for, Lord;
> You hear my every sigh. (Ps. 38:9, NLT)

And lead us not into temptation,
but deliver us from the evil one. (Mt. 6:13, NIV)

Because you know that the testing of your faith produces perseverance. (Jms. 6:13, NIV)

Brothers and sisters, if someone is caught in a sin, you who live by the Spirit should restore that person gently. But watch yourselves, or you also may be tempted. (Gal. 6:1, NIV)

For we do not have a high priest who is unable to sympathize with our weaknesses, but one who in every respect has been tempted as we are, yet without sin. (Heb. 4:15, ESV)

The seed falling among the thorns refers to someone who hears the word, but the worries of this life and the deceitfulness of wealth choke the word, making it unfruitful. (Mt. 13:22, NIV)

Therefore put on the full armor of God, so that when the day of evil comes, you may be able to stand your ground, and after you have done everything, to stand. (Eph. 6:13, NIV)

Instead, clothe yourselves with the Lord Jesus Christ, make no provision for the flesh, to gratify its desires. (Rom. 13:14, ESV)

If this is so, then the Lord knows how to rescue the godly from trials and to hold the unrighteous for punishment on the day of judgment. (2 Pet. 2:9, NIV)

Jesus, full of the Holy Spirit, left the Jordan and was led by the Spirit into the wilderness, where for forty days he was tempted by the devil. He ate nothing during those days, and at the end of them he was hungry. (Lk. 4:1-2, NIV)

As you can see, there are waaayyyy more scriptures surrounding temptation. That's because we need to be warned that the roach **will** come for us, whether we fast or not, and what better time for him to tempt us then when we are at our weakest physically. he knows full well that our flesh is tainted by sin and wants comfort. he tried it with Jesus, why wouldn't he try it with us? But we can take solace that God will not let us get tempted past what we can handle. He has already made a way out.

Fasting is practice for denying our flesh. If we can deny ourselves in this practical but very important way, we will have gained strength to do the same in other areas of our lives.

THE FAST PLAN

1. First, pray and seek the Lord on what you should be fasting from. Food is obviously number one from a

biblical standpoint, but I know from experience that there are many other things that were a struggle for me that had to be added onto the food fast. Also, if you cannot medically fast, this provides a way to also seek the Lord. I have heard of miracles that come out of fasting for three hours a day. God accepts it all!

2. Second, based on the leading of the Holy Spirit, make a list of Do's and Don'ts. For the "all juice" fast, we made sure to add things like no added sugars, only things that come from the Earth can go to a juice or a soup, and it must be liquid. We allowed things like spices, pepper, etc. We also made a list for acceptable programming, times to pray, and we had an accountability group chat. Do what you need to do to succeed.

3. Third, go shopping. There is nothing worse than making that list and not having the ingredients you need to succeed. Get the things you need for the fast, look at labels, delete the apps you need to delete, make sure you have your accountability partner's phone numbers, or if you're fasting alone, put reminders on your phone to remind yourself that you're fasting, times of prayer, get your Bible ready, etc. Only you and God know your weaknesses, so seek Him in these steps. Ultimately, set yourself up for success.

4. Fourth, document how the Lord is moving in your life during this fast. For us, we used the group chat as a point of reference, but I also journal. It's honestly amazing to be able to look back and see God's faithfulness.

5. Last but not least, pray! Put on the whole armor of God. (Eph. 6:10-18) This is the entire point of fasting. We are opening up communication lines with our Lord and Savior in ways we have never seen before. We are drawing closer to Him so we can build our relationship with and understand our dependance on Him. Ultimately, petty prayer is simply depending on Him for our every need. So when you pray, you don't need to talk to him in King James, be real with Him. He already knows your needs. If you're hungry that day and your mother brought your favorite food over for no reason, let Him know how trifling she was and that You love her anyway. (You can clearly tell this is my story, he he). Be real with Him. The all-powerful God doesn't want to just be your dad, He wants to be your friend.

Cleanse Your Mind

Step 2

"How much more will the blood of Christ, who through
the eternal Spirit offered Himself without blemish to God,
leans your conscience from dead works to serve the living
God"~ Hebrews 9:14

In the age of social media and as a millennial myself, I realize that we are so overwhelmed with information that it's hard to keep tabs on the emotional roller coaster it creates in our mental, physical, and emotional health, and ultimately our walk with God. Cleansing your mind goes hand in hand with fasting. When I fasted with those ladies, we also decided to cleanse our minds by staying off social media, only watching God-related programming and staying in our Word. This brings us to my third point, which we'll discuss a little later.

Cleansing your mind is about being truthful with yourself. What do you struggle with that doesn't align with the Word of God or your conscience? What can you give up during this time that can start a pathway into more constructive habits that glorify God? I have found that when I put those habits on the altar, God was faithful to help break the habit altogether. Sometimes He even broke habits I didn't even know were a problem.

Here are some practical ways you can cleanse your mind:

1. Take a break from online shopping
2. Stop watching TV
3. Focus on reading your Word and watching Bible videos
4. Watch movies on Pureflix or another Christian-based platform.
5. Give up video games (looking at you all you "Call of Duty" fanatics)
6. Get off social media (now this one is a very important one, there is just too much information on social media competing for your time with God)
7. Turn off news notifications (this is one I missed sometimes, but it's a big one; these news outlets strive to drive fear and anger for ratings)
8. Set a time each day just to spend time with God
9. Talk to God like He is your friend (because He is)
10. Believe that all this means something. This is very important. The roach likes to make our efforts seem pointless. Even if you mess up, God sees your heart. Just repent and continue on. God meets you where you are. He will move in the fact that you are trying.

For my fast, different women fasted in different ways. I did the more intense fast with just juicing, but some people ate at 6 pm, some got off of social media for a time, but all of us were in our Word and constantly in communication with each other and holding each other accountable. We failed so many times, especially during our first fast.

However, we noticed that when we had a plan, there were way fewer hiccups.

The habits I formed during the fast have stuck with me well after. I barely watch any television, I fast weekly, my Amazon addiction is gone, and I honestly don't even really have a desire for these things anymore. God knows exactly what He's doing.

The Itsy Bitsy Spider

One day a spider that looked like a baby tarantula came into my house. Y'all, I looked away for one second, and in an instant it disappeared. That was the worst feeling ever! I was paranoid for a while and felt like at any moment it might end up on my face, my leg, or somewhere else. I hate that feeling.

Anywhoo, I forgot about it, and a week later, I heard my husband shout, "How did something like that get in here?" I immediately knew what he was talking about.

Because I hadn't taken care of it, it came back and became someone else's problem (sounds like a picture of generational issues to me). At this point, Tony took his rightful place as king of my home and resident bug killer and handled his business. In all honesty, we weren't sure if it was a baby tarantula or not at the time, especially since we don't live in a place where those types of insects are prevalent. We did some research and it ended up being some other spider that looked like a tarantula. It was the tiniest thing that caused a whole lot of commotion in the house. It didn't even end up being a baby tarantula.

It was just ugly and weird, and we were 100 times its size. It was dead in a matter of moments. I told Tony that day that whenever a bug comes into my house, it's asking for death.

It needs to stay in its lane. I won't bother it outside, but it had entered my house and needed to die.

The Holy Spirit made me realize how prophetic that was. If it entered my house... it needed to die. Unlike spiders, who most of the time take up residence in your home because they just happened to wander in and found bugs they could eat, roaches come to invade, steal, kill, and destroy. Sound familiar? And they are always looking for ways to leech off you, to eat your food, and carry all sorts of diseases.

This is what clouding our minds with unfruitful information does to our walk with God. It's not only a distraction but a poison that kills us slowly. You see, the eyes are the window to the soul (Pr. 30:17). What better way for the roach to invade than to come for something that is directly connected to your soul? Even though some of these are not of themselves sinful, not all are fruitful, especially if they are taking away our time, which is already short.

> *"All things are lawful, but not all things are profitable. All things are lawful, but not all things edify." (1 Cor. 10:23)*

Read Your Word

Step 3: Through His Word

"How much more will the blood of Christ, who through the eternal Spirit offered Himself without blemish to God, cleanse your conscience from dead works to serve the living God"~ Hebrews 9:14

To get to know someone, we take them out to dinner, talk on the phone and they tell us about their likes, dislikes, what their favorite color is, what their biggest pet peeve is, how to make them happy and what grieves them. If we want to get to know God, we have to dive into His Word.ss

God speaks to us through the greatest love letter that's been ever written: The Bible. It is the best story ever told. The story of how much He loves us. Examples of times that people made Him angry and He had to handle it, but also times He just had to let bygones be bygones because He's just so full of love. (Ps. 103)

God's Words are life-changing Words. The Bible is living. It reads you as much as you read it. You will find out things about yourself that you never knew, but also, it will bring you to a place where you have pure evidence of God's hand in other people's lives. It builds your faith to see God work through imperfect people just like us.

I know this is hard for some people, especially because bills don't stop needing to be paid while you fast and as you get closer to God but if you put Him first, you will see everything start to work together. Not to say that there won't be opposition because the roach will try everything in his power to distract, discourage, and confuse you, but don't give up. You have got the God of the universe on your side.

When I first started reading the Bible, I understood literally nothing. Yes, I had the basics from the times I had spent at church growing up, but when I got to some of the hard parts of the Bible, especially in the Old Testament, I could've scratched my head for days.

But something happened to me as a new Christian. I just decided I would believe and the explanation for the things I didn't understand or agree with would come to me. That was the best decision I ever made, especially since I was twenty-one years old at the time and full of opinions. God met me in my ignorance just because I was willing to believe even when I didn't understand.

> *"My thoughts are nothing like your thoughts," says the Lord. "And my ways are far beyond anything you could imagine" (Is. 55:8)*

Get to Know God

Step 4: He is the Same

"Jesus Christ is the same yesterday and today and for-ever."~ Hebrews 13:8

I know we touched on how to get to know God in the last chapter, but I have to emphasize this point. Even if I have to use a whole chapter heading for a few paragraphs. A lot of us, myself included, kind of put God's miracles in a time of just the Bible. But if God is the same yesterday, today, and forever, that means He is the same God who splits seas, heals the sick, casts out demons, and defeats all your enemies for you. He is the same God who created the heavens and the Earth, and He has not changed. If we are not as close to God as we once were, we are the ones who moved.

Yes, God does things for different seasons and can speak to everyone 's culture and mind in different ways, but He is the same. He has not lost power over time. In fact, He is not even subject to time. He lives outside of time and entered time as Jesus just to save us. Oh, how great is our God.

Learn How to Fight

Step 5: Stand in your authority

"Pray Continually."~ 1 Thessalonians 5:17

We are at war, whether you choose to ignore the grenades and rocket launchers flying outside or not. And no, this is not "Call of Duty" where you have multiple lives. You have one, but... Jesus did buy you back, so there's that. With buying you back, though, He bought you back with superpowers. He gave you the same power that He has as the ultimate superhero. Then He said, "I want you to come live with Me in My neighborhood where My streets are paved with gold."

Like I said, fighting against fellow image bearers is usually a pointless battle. Even if you know full well that the person is fully moving in conjunction with the enemy, we must learn to fight against the enemy behind them and pray against the behavior. Honestly, some people may never change, but God is the ultimate judge of that. You would be very surprised at how many people are fully oblivious to the fact that they are the problem. The devil and his demons have gotten them so fooled. Besides, those who have fully committed to living as the roach's child will receive their just reward. We must ask God for the wisdom to reconcile praying for *and* against our enemies at the same time. Like I've said before, a lot of times our Lord asks us to have two seemingly opposite postures at the same time. The best and most potent weapon you can have is to give them to God. "God will grant his chosen ones justice and quickly." *(Lk. 18:8, NIV)*

Much like my childhood self, many of us are under the impression that if you leave the roach alone, he'll leave you alone. Let me ask you this: Does an actual roach leave you alone? Don't they just creep in unexpectedly and try to leech off the sustenance of your house? Oh, you can ignore it for a little while, when you think it's not that bad, until those nasty vermin are crawling on your dishes and you're just trying to have dinner in your house in peace.

In the same way, it is better to take preventative measures. Before the roach even thinks about looking your way, be armed up to win in prayer. The best way to look at it is: roaches always want to move in. Demons, principalities in high places and all things under that pest's umbrella are always going to want to come and destroy your relationship with God. It's inevitable. The Bible says that he "prowls around like a lion looking for whom he may devour." *(1 Pet. 5:8)*

He is an unsatisfied, mangy lion that has nothing better to do than try to cause strife in your life. Once we understand that there is nothing we can do to change the roach's character, we will begin to understand how much we need to fight and make our lives uninhabitable to the roach. he is always coming for anything good so we must be armed up with roach repellent aka a potent prayer life. Now I don't say this to have you worrying and looking over your shoulder at every turn. We must be on guard but also in authority. Know that you have an enemy, but also understand that as Christians, we are fighting from a place of victory. Le roach has already lost. If we can truly recognize that he is fighting with one hand tied behind his back, and that we have the ultimate Champion on our side fighting for us, it will give us the confidence to always go to God preemptively. Too many Christians are praying in defense when we need to be praying in offense. It's much easier to repel roaches and have them never enter your home than to have to hire an exterminator or do one of those Raid drownings or sandal overkills. You know, the times when you use up the entire roach spray bottle or smack it 37 times with our shoe, just to be sure.

Also, God is not some far away God who doesn't care about the petty details of our lives. He is so intimately involved in every single portion of our lives that He cares about things that we don't even care about. Again, He numbers the hairs on our heads. Better yet, He knows how many finger clippings we've ever thrown in the garbage. Yeah, once we acknowledge how deeply He cares about us, we will be way more open and willing to have Him fight our battles for us.

This is something I still struggle with at times. Like I said, God is still working on me. However, whenever I struggle to trust Him, I can go back to the times He has kept me before. The times when He has moved miraculously before. I can praise Him for those times and in advance for the things I ask for and for His protection, because if I am praying in accordance with His will, everything is mine. Everything is yours. If it is already part of His plan for you, and He wants it for you, "Who can stand against you"? *(Ps. 27)*

Now I feel like I have to reiterate "His" will. Not yours. Yes, your feelings and wants are valid, but the goal of this Christian life is that we eventually become so intertwined with God that our will is His will. He reconciled us through Jesus' atonement on the cross. However, He wants us to willingly give up our will for His. I know it's tough, huh. Especially when telling Sheila off at the office is well deserved and God wants you to kill her with kindness instead. Whew, Lord. That's a tough one, but you know what? There's nothing better than to show Sheila and her crazy self love while Jesus deals with her nonsense. There is nothing in my opinion that is more petty.

Our will must become aligned with God, and the only way that happens is if we figure out what His will is. The way we do that is to read our Bible and listen to the promptings of the Holy Spirit. The Holy Spirit is our Helper. The one Jesus left to guide us.

If we look at Jesus, His will was always to do the will of "His father in Heaven."

> ***For I have come down from heaven, not to do my own will but the will of Him who sent Me. (Jn. 6:38)***

Watch Your Mouth

The Power of Life and Death is in the Tongue

"The power of life and death is in the tongue"~
Proverbs 18:21

There is so much power in the words we say. We are made in the image of our Heavenly Father. If God has created us in His image. it means we're His copies. He has given us the same power from the beginning to bring life, to have dominion, and to be His representatives here on Earth. In the beginning, He said, "Let us make them in our image." It's like drawing a real life painting. When drawing a portrait of someone we look at their eyes, mouths, noses, bone structure, complexion and everything else to try to make the painting look like the original.

God is the great painter. Not only did he create us to look like him soul, body and spirit, but there is so much more! He wanted us to look like Him in every way even in the authority of our speech. He created us to be just like Jesus. In the beginning, God spoke and said, "Let there be light," and there was light. If He has painted us to walk like Him, talk like Him, and move like Him, why wouldn't our words hold weight like Him?

Unfortunately, we live in a broken world and our words have that weight, whether we speak life or death into our lives, over people, or into any situation. And the roach knows it. he is cognizant of the power our words hold and will hop right on it to "make that wish come true." he loves it when we lie to ourselves. he is the father of lies. It's why he whispers horrible things into our ears. If we are constantly repeating negativity, we will bring negativity into our lives. If we live in fear, we will become fear.

Look at the life of Jesus. He was able to calm the seas with His Words. What if I told you that you could do that too? Our God said we will do even greater things than these! *(Jn. 14:12)* I don't know about you, but I take Jesus at His Word, and I'm trying to feed 10,000 people with a protein bar that turns into a steak. I'm a little extra, I know, but I'm low key serious. **Have Big Faith!**

Speak life into your situation, not death. If someone speaks death over any aspect of your life, rebuke it. You don't have to do it out loud (like I do all the time), but it can be something as simple as rebuking them under your breath. That roach and his roach-ettes have very good hearing.

> *"We are destroying speculations and every lofty thing raised up against the knowledge of God, and we are taking every thought captive to the obedience of Christ." (2 Cor. 10:5)*

The reason this step is here is because people will proclaim curses over you and have you believing it. What a lot of people don't know is that having faith in something that brings death into your situation is the equivalent to having faith and bringing life into a situation.

Whether you are saved by Christ or not, you are made in His image. There was no prerequisite and your tongue has the same power. He spoke this very world into existence, and we can speak things into existence as well. Now I'm not speaking from some weird new age standpoint, but simply from what the Word of God says about humanity. You can bring bad things into fruition just like you can bring good things. We must learn to mirror God's Word over every single situation, big or small, because the small things add up.

Think of it this way: having one dollar can probably get you some chips from a store nowadays, if that. That dollar isn't worth much on its own, but having a million of those dollars can buy you a whole house. Now think about this: what if that dollar represented someone calling you ugly. Once may have an effect on you, depending on the weight that person holds in your life, but for the sake of the example, let's make the person who said it a jokester friend. If they said it one time in a joke, no biggie, you know it was a joke. But what if they started saying it every day in front of people, really making fun of you, describing why you're ugly and that you will never be in a relationship because of it. Wouldn't that take a toll on your self-esteem? If you didn't know you were fearfully and wonderfully made, wouldn't it kill the image you had of yourself? This is the exact tactic used by the roach. If he can say it enough times, and get you to start repeating it, you have more faith in the fact that you think you are ugly than that you are wonderfully made by God. How many seemingly petty things happen to us in this way?

This is why it's important to read your Word. When Jesus was tempted in the desert, He used God's Word to come against the devil's temptations. The roach may even try to use God's Word against you, like he did with Jesus, and just like slave owners did during slavery but if you are constantly reading your Bible you can combat the lies of the enemy. Perversion of God's Word is definitely one of the roach's main MO's. If he can get you to doubt what God said with something taken completely out of context, he has got you duped.

We have been given authority through Christ Jesus. He has even given us the ability to move mountains (Mt. 17:20). We must use our tongues to speak life and not death into every single situation. No matter if that's someone's actual life or the fact that you need to breathe life into this light turning green really quick so that you can get to your Zoom meeting on time (definitely a pandemic joke, but you get the gist).

> *"But I tell you that every careless word that people speak, they shall give an accounting for it in the day of judgement."*
> *(Mt. 12:36)*

Get a P.I.P.P.
Partner In Petty Prayer

"A Lion does not turn around when a dog barks"~
African Proverb

I have been extremely blessed to have been put in a situation where I have a husband and fellow brothers and sisters in Christ who understand the power in casting our cares on Jesus, and can stand with me in prayer. It wasn't always that way. I was isolated for a very long time, but honestly, it was God setting me apart.

If you look at the Bible, there are many such examples where God's prophets have felt isolated and misunderstood. Even our Lord felt that way. The Word says He had to stay in lonely places. But honestly, God is our ultimate friend. It is important to find a body, but honestly, sometimes God will have you isolated. It won't always feel great, but even Jesus had twelve disciples but chose three of them to be closest to Him. Then He went off by Himself in the middle of the night. If we are honest with ourselves, we can feel isolated in a crowd of people. I say all that to say that we were made for one another. We were made to carry one another's burdens, and for iron to sharpen iron. We need one another, we need to pray in groups, people to love on us, and for us to love on them. We need to have give and take relationships. Godly community is very important, even when we don't think it is.

But if you don't yet have that group, take courage that Jesus is the friend you always needed. The friend who will never let you down or betray you. The friend who knows you inside and out. Sometimes, feeling isolated is God teaching you to be alone and not being lonely. God knows exactly what you need in the season you are in, and believe that He will send you friends like He has sent me. Sometimes, I look at these people and wonder how I even befriended them, but I couldn't imagine doing life without them, their prayers, their faults and all their shenanigans, because God didn't give me the friends I wanted, He gave me the friends and husband I needed.

Tony

I have to mention my ultimate PIPP. My husband, my ride or die, the best friend God gave me. The father to my child and the royal pain in my butt. Yes, I had to ruin it. I thank God for him. I thank God that I have a husband who doesn't think I'm crazy when God is guiding me into all kinds of crazy situations. I like to call them Holy Shenanigans.

For example, I decided to take Tony on a luxury birthday trip to the Cayman Islands. That vacation wore many hats since it ended up being a birthday/baby moon/competition finisher since I had at least tried to top my surprise birthday trip to Europe, and I was about six months pregnant. Little did I know that God was going to have us on another holy adventure that day.

So, like all millennials, we sort of underestimated the time it would take to get to the airport and through TSA. To be fair, we grew up with Caribbean parents who would arrive at the airport at 3 am for a 9 am flight. We were not going to follow in their footsteps, but we assumed that three hours was enough time. Boy, were we wrong. We were running a little late, but we weren't late enough that we wouldn't make the flight. Then traffic hit. I don't know what got into me when I scheduled our flight out of another state, but I wanted to be fancy and get Tony a first class ticket, which wasn't available to that location in my state. Hmm, I guess our competitive nature is what got into me. Ah, that silly married life competition, but I digress. We hit a whole lot of traffic on the way and we ended up getting to the airport about an hour before our flight was set to depart. Mind you, we had not even gone through TSA yet and were flapping around trying to make our flight.

We met with what I assumed was a TSA agent in the front of the line to get in and showed her our tickets, where she said, "You are not going to make it." We hadn't even checked our bags yet. I always make it a point not to check a bag, but Tony's clothes and shoes are much bigger than mine, so he always checks one. The woman at the front told us they had already boarded our flight and we had missed it. Sigh. The representative pointed us toward the customer service line so we could try to exchange our tickets for another flight.

Side note: I decided to get a ticket where I could freely exchange without paying a fee because I know God likes to disrupt my regularly scheduled programming and I was trying to not pay a fee. Also, during my pregnancy I felt amazing! God had His hand on me where I had no MS symptoms whatsoever even before I got pregnant. Usually it is hard for me to stand for long periods of time, but I felt amazing and that line was a piece of cake.

Anyway, as we were in this extremely long customer service line in the middle of the airport, a woman got on the line a good ways away from me, yelling. She was an older woman and she was having a heated disagreement with her mother. I found it strange since, this was already an older woman herself. I was a bit curious as to what a possibly eighty-plus woman could be saying to make her that angry, but I decided it was none of my business.

Until it was...

I kid you not, she was far enough behind me that she wasn't extremely close, but for some reason the Lord positioned it so that as we moved along the queue, she would be right next to me on the opposite side of the ropes that separated the lines. And every time she got close to me, she got louder. The first time, I didn't think anything of it. The second time, I said in my heart, "Lord, what is going on here?" The third time, I was like, Okay, God is about to be funky today," but I didn't know what He wanted me to do. I still just wanted to get on my flight to the Caymans and be on my way. The whole time, I didn't know it, but God was talking to Tony, too.

We finally got to the front and the customer service agent explained that there was only one flight out to the Cayman Islands a day. Let's just say, in the words of the great Pastor Tony Evans, I was a little "evangelically ticked off." I wasn't angry per se, but I was kind of annoyed. The representative was really nice and tried her hardest to get us seats that were next to each other in first class. She got us similar seats so we could just ask the person on the other side of the window seat to switch places with us. We agreed and thanked God that we could still be in first class, and that we didn't have to pay a fee to switch flights.

As the agent was finishing up with us, I looked over and I saw that same woman break out into tears and run off. I was thinking, "Okay, God, what do You want me to do?" She ran off and I didn't even see where she went. As I was just looking around, the line was just as packed, and it was a big-city airport. How was I supposed to find her? And also, I had no idea what I was supposed to do, anyway.

As Tony and I walked toward the back so we could get a cab and begin to head our way back home, I saw the woman, let's call her Sally, sitting on the floor on the phone with her mom, still visibly and audibly angry. I knew I had to help her, but I wasn't sure what was going on. I started to walk past her when I felt the Holy Spirit say, "So you're just going to walk past her?" Nope. Not at all. Not after I just got stopped by God. When God speaks, I listen, period. Especially when it's that loud in my spirit. I stopped dead in my tracks.

This was where Tony came in. He had been walking a little bit ahead of me since he was rolling both our bags. I went up to him and said, "Babe, do you mind if we help her?"

Now y'all, sometimes I get all types of embarrassed when I'm about to tell Tony that we're about to be on another shenanigan. I don't know why, maybe because it happens so often and it's always at times like this when we're both tired, hungry, and I'm pregnant. I mean, I'm not always pregnant, but you get the gist. He turned around and said, "Sure!"

At this point, I had to figure out how to help her. So, I see a woman standing at the podium. Let's call her TSA Agent Grace. I walked up to Agent Grace, who was also visibly pregnant. That fact is not important, but I thought it was funny. So I walked up to Agent Grace and asked her if there was an ATM nearby. I wasn't sure what was going on, but I overheard Sally talking about money. Agent Grace told me there was one on the far end of the airport. And this airport was an airport in one of the biggest cities in the country. It was not a small task to travel that far. Even though MS took a back seat during my pregnancy, I was still very pregnant. Then Agent Grace asked me what I needed the cash for. My response, although I'm not proud of it, it was real. I said, "I'm trying to help the crazy lady." She chuckled. I asked her what the problem was, and she told me that Sally couldn't pay for her bags or something.

I asked Agent Grace how much it was, and it was something like $30. Agent Grace then told me I could just pay for her at the service desk. She went to pull some strings while I went to talk to Sally. I headed over, and she was just stuck, not knowing how she was going to get out of the situation. I said "Ma'am" a couple times before she even heard me. She was still on the phone with her mom and visibly in distress. I told her I wanted to help her, and her face just lit up. She didn't look like she thought anyone would help her.

Agent Grace pulled some strings and got us to the front of the line with a representative who was finishing up with another customer. During that time, Sally and I were talking, and without going into too much detail, she shared some life situations with me and shared that she was trying to get down south to visit her mother.

I just talked to her and realized that she was just a woman in a tough spot with external and internal pressures, and that made her react in ways she wasn't proud of. I related with her, because everyone goes through something in this life, and if I were going through the things she was going through,

I would be a bit upset too. Heck, I was not very happy that I missed my flight that morning, but God knew what He was doing. He needed me there to help that woman. Now we got to the front and the agent told me it was not her bags she couldn't afford, it was the change in flight that she missed, and that it was a bit more expensive. Facepalm.

Oh, you mean the change in flight that I didn't have to pay for myself? That same amount that I had just saved on my own missed flight? Ah. Okay. The representative asked me if I still wanted to pay it. Yes, I still wanted to pay it. This was clearly God's doing. I was already there and Sally needed to get to her mom. After we were done, Sally and I said goodbye to one another.

I finally got a chance to look up after being in Holy Spirit Adventure mode, and all eyes were on me for some reason. Oddly, people did tend to stare at me, but I always thought it was because I have these huge dolls eyes. This felt different, but I shrugged it off and headed to Tony.

This whole time, Grace and Tony were having a conversation while Tony was waiting for me to finish up the payment with Sally.

By this time, I was hungry. I didn't have cravings during my pregnancy, but this kid had to eat. We had decided to go to Dunkin Donuts. While Tony and I are talking about getting food, Grace walked up to us and said her coworker wanted to speak to us.

Huh.

Lord, I'm hungry, but okay. We head over to where Grace told us she was, and she was a security guard who had seen the whole thing transpire. She said it moved her and she wanted to help us when we came back tomorrow. She gave me her number and I took it without thinking anything of it.

We got our food and headed back home to tell my parents, who were house sitting, the whole story. They were amazed.

The next morning, we woke up much earlier because we were not going through that again, but there was sleet and ice everywhere. We were like, "Lord, do we stay home or something? I mean, You could have told us before we spent all this money, Sir." But we felt the green light to go, so we got in the Uber and he got us there safely. I called the security guard, not really knowing what was up, and she came to us. Y'all, she breezed us through the entire process. We were in and out of the TSA in like ten minutes. They did all the checks, but we were straight up VIP. It happened so fast that my head spun. As we were going through the lines, the lady who told us we had missed our flight said, "Yes, they deserve this treatment." Y'all, I didn't even know people were watching. I don't like helping people for people to see. I made sure to be very careful in how loudly I spoke because I didn't want to draw any attention to it.

But apparently, Sally drew a lot of attention to herself. As I was sitting in the waiting area to get on my flight, with enough time to get breakfast and go through my prayer list for the trip, I pondered on what happened these past two days.

I pondered on the fact that everyone did what every other person from a big city does when there's a standard "crazy" person yelling in a public place: we ignore it. We write them off as someone who we want nothing to do with. We only pay attention in case something crazy happens or we have to defend ourselves or run away, but that is the extent of it. Sally was dismissed because she was someone who was in distress.

A lot of times, I feel like I'm the only one who sees the homeless in need. Sally needed help, and because she was deemed as "crazy," no one would step out of their comfort zone to help her. In all honesty, I was also convicted because I really just wanted to go, and my own feelings almost got in the way of me blessing someone also.

A lot of times, even we as Christians can get so caught up in the hustle and bustle of the day and getting things done the way we want to do it that we will miss a learning opportunity with God, and miss an opportunity to represent Him.

Everyone on that line, everyone who heard her, whoever was told of the story, knew God was good that day. One of the things Agent Grace said to me was, "God bless you." I didn't even have to tell her that I was a Christian, she already knew by my behavior. It was already written all over what I was doing. The simple fact that I decided to help someone like Sally showed that I served something greater than myself. It was spoken and unspoken all at the same time.

As I waited for my flight to board and looked at my prayer list with the million hours of time that I now had, I had forgotten these two prayers. One was, "represent God wherever I go," and the other was "to breeze through the TSA." I had a host of prayers for that trip and God answered them all. We had favor with everyone we came in contact with. We had a great room. Even the weather worked in our favor. We returned safe and sound. There were no flight cancellations. And I even learned that the person I switched my seat with was sick, and the woman who ended up sitting next to him, whom I had a lovely conversation with before and had ended up on our returning flight as well, said she got sick with something that she couldn't explain. In all honesty, I think that man had COVID and God saved me from getting the coronavirus while pregnant. God saw my entire prayer list and just started checking the little boxes off on my phone.

Now how is this a story about Tony? Some husbands would get in the way. Tony was just as tired and hungry as I was. He had missed the same flight. Heard that same lady yelling, spent the same amount of time in the line, all while worrying about his pregnant wife. Also, this was his birthday trip. When I told him I wanted to help someone who was visibly in distress, he could have gone into self-preservation mode over himself, his wife and his unborn child, but instead, he knew we had to do the right thing. He also listened to the Holy Spirit, and he trusted that God would protect me while I did His will. He was not only there, but he was an integral part of the day. He believed that God spoke to me. He held the bags, and y'all, we're married, that was his money that I spent too.

I thank God for a husband like Tony, who I can talk to regarding my faith. Even when he doesn't quite understand my relationship with God sometimes, he has his own and I can always depend on the fact that he will at least hear me out. I know we can pray together when things get rough and when things are good. I know we have similar hearts when it comes to helping people. I know that whenever a holy shenanigan arises, even when it gets in the way of his plans, he knows that God is the first person in our relationship and I will do whatever God says, as will he.

Having a partner in petty prayer is important, especially in your spouse, because they are the one God gave you for the rest of your life. Friends may go, children will grow up and leave for their own lives, but your partner is that permanent best friend God fashioned just for you. I thank God for him, even when he gets on my nerves, because in all honesty, I wouldn't have it any other way.

If you and your spouse don't currently see eye to eye spiritually, pray for God to open up their hearts. Pray continually, because your relationship with God and each other will mold your children. Tony and I weren't always these "Super Christians," as people like to think. We went through a lot of trials in our relationship, especially surrounding God, because we started off our relationship in the world and when God comes to take over in a relationship, get ready for a bumpy ride. But, God in all His sovereignty, in the middle of our dirt, in the middle of us not doing the right thing and being ignorant children, teens, and even being ignorant in our marriage, knew the plans He had for us.

God Shows UP!

Pay attention to the things we cannot explain.

I felt the need to let you know: The supernatural is real. It has to be. How else did Jesus feed 5,000 people (literally like twice) with two fish and five loaves of bread? How else did He miraculously and instantly heal people? Or better yet, how did homeboy come back from the dead? A lot of people, even Christians, would say that the supernatural is no longer a thing and that people do not hear God's voice. I'm here to tell you that this little girl from Brooklyn, who was scared of her shadow, scared of the dark, scared to take a shower alone because of the roach, this was her very calling. I was created to move in the supernatural and have all sorts of holy shenanigans and to be God's representative to people.

I'm going to share a story that happened with my other PIPP. My gorgeous and crazy best friend, Fabie.

COFFEE BREAK

Gather around kids… I have another story to tell.

As I have said before, God always has me on some sort of holy shenanigan. This story I'm about to tell you is one for the books.

On the anniversary of said shenanigan, my God felt it necessary that I share this testimony.

My parents' house

It was a regular Sunday on June 30th, 2019. Well, technically, it wasn't wholly ordinary. My parents had asked me to help them set up their Roku TV devices for streaming. So, I decided to stop by my parents' house before church to fulfill my millennial child duties. As we all know, millennials are their parents' private technicians and No is not an option.

Anyway, it worked out that I could meet up with my best friend Fabie, who was a few short blocks away at her father's church. We decided to head to our church together after I was done helping my parents.

And yes… she went to two churches, LOL. #super saved.

My husband Tony dropped me off and then headed off to a suit fitting with Fabie's then-future husband. He and I would meet after church at Ippudo Ramen in NY (I love that place). We had invited a couple of friends to church and wanted to catch up with them afterward. I would ride with our friends to the restaurant and meet Tony, as he was already in the city. I thought what better place to catch up than over some delicious chicken buns.

Ah Ippudo, how I miss thee...

Between explaining to my parents how to use the devices and a problem setting up one of them, I spent nearly three hours helping them. I decided to come back another day to set up the final device, as I wanted to hang out with Fabie a little bit as well as get to church on time. I was already about thirty minutes late meeting her. So, I kissed my mom and dad goodbye and walked toward Flatbush, where I had promised to meet her. When we saw each other, it felt like we hadn't seen each other in years.

Hanging out was special

We hung out almost every Sunday after church. However, it was a hectic time helping her plan her wedding. My husband and I were chosen to be matron of honor and best man, so we were swamped, especially since their wedding was just a few short months away. It had been a while since we could just hang out sans wedding talk. I was happy to get this time with her even if it was just for an hour or so before church.

Then it starts...

As usual, when Fabie and I got together, we talked and giggled like two school girls.

We decided to go to a Haitian restaurant next door to her father's church to have a quick bite to eat, then take a dollar van downtown. We both had dinner plans later, but we were hungry. Also, who could pass up Haitian food?

We walked into the restaurant and placed our order for a plate of Fritaye (basically Haitian appetizers). We didn't want to overeat as we knew we would be eating later on. That day was a revival at her dad's church, and as mentioned before, I was saving room for that Ramen. We decided to take it to go since we were already a little behind schedule. We paid for our order at the counter as we continued to chat.

Waiting for our food

When Fabie and I get together, we get lost in conversation. We talked about everything from Jesus to childhood memories. While at the counter, we stopped in mid-conversation, as we started to realize that this was taking longer than we anticipated.

"They are usually much quicker than this," Fabie said, as we decided to sit down and wait on our food.

At this point, we were going to be late but not by much. Worship was probably still going on, so we had time to at least get there for the sermon. We sat and continued to talk. Another thirty minutes passed by with no update, so I asked Fabie to find out what was going on. They informed us that the food was on its way. We decided to wait, as by this point we were starving and had already paid for our food.

As we sat and waited, I looked at Fabie and said, "Girl, I don't think we're going to church today." I assumed that there was some reason, but I still had to go downtown to meet the friends Tony and I had invited, even if we only made it for the after-church socializing.

A few moments later, a lady came out from the kitchen (whom we assumed was the cook) and informed us that our food should be finished shortly and that they were pressing the plantains… **What?**

Okay, so clearly something was up, as plantains took forever to press and fry. How could they just have started? We weren't sure what was going on yet, but we figured we could still meet up with people after church, right?

Our food got to us a whole twenty minutes after we spoke with the lady. We ate and talked about how weird this was feeling. We thought, "Okay, Jesus, what are You protecting us from?"

On our way to church

We left the restaurant thinking that it was strange, but assumed that God just wanted to delay us from whatever danger was going on at the time. After all, we were trying to go to church. If there was ever anything God wouldn't get in the way of, it was His children trying to go to church, right?

Never, and I mean never, assume things about God.

Like I mentioned before, Fabie and I decided to take a dollar van down Flatbush to our church to save time. If you know something about Flatbush Avenue in Brooklyn:

There is always a dollar van.

Keep that in mind.

Fabie wrapped up our leftovers and we left the restaurant. We headed to the bodega a couple of stores down where I withdrew $20 from the ATM, since we needed cash for the dollar van. As most people in Brooklyn are aware, dollar vans prefer exact change. The quickest way to get money thrown at you is to hand a dollar van driver a twenty dollar bill that they have to make change for at a traffic light.

Needless to say, I decided to buy some chewing gum to break up the twenty dollar bill. The man behind the counter proceeded to hand me the difference in a bunch of small bills. Like I wanted change, but the number of bills he handed me was obnoxious. I thought it was weird, but I took the change, and we were on our way.

Dollar vans

While we were waiting for a dollar van to pull up on the corner, Fabie and I continued to talk about how weird the restaurant thing was, but we thanked God for whatever He prevented from happening to us by delaying our trip. After about twenty-five minutes, we realized:

No dollar vans were coming down Flatbush.

Strange.

We waited a few more minutes, but something was definitely up.

"God is being funky," I said. "We're just trying to go to church, Jesus. Why is this so hard?"

We laughed, but both of us figured: *Okay, maybe He doesn't want us on dollar vans.*

They weren't the safest forms of transportation anyway. Both Fabie and I come from culturally overly cautious Haitian parents who always advised us that if God was getting in the way, it was for a reason. We mostly dismissed their advice as being worrisome but, I mean, it was clear He snatched up all the dollar vans so we didn't get on.

"Let's try the train," I said.

Fabie agreed. As we walked toward the train, we were laughing nervously but also just laughing because we knew in our hearts that we were literally in the hands of the Holy Spirit at this point.

God Himself had officially hijacked our evening.

Walking toward the train

As we walked down Flatbush Avenue toward Flatbush Junction, we passed a homeless lady sitting on a bench. I instantly felt pulled to her. However, I ignored it as I wasn't sure what was happening and wanted to stay alert. At that moment, the only dollar van we had seen since this whole ordeal began pulled up to us, and I kid you not, the man opened up the door and said:

"There are no seats for you."

He closed the door, and we looked at each other like, welp... guess the Lord just confirmed that He didn't want us to get on a dollar van today. Like, who opens up a dollar van just to tell you that there are no seats? (facepalm).

Fabie and I walked to the train station, which was only about half a block away. We reached the top of the train station, and we were both stopped dead in our tracks.

We had no idea what was happening. We looked down at the steps and then looked over at each other simultaneously, when Fabie said, "You can't go in there, can you?"

"No!" I replied, confused. We were spiritually blocked from going down those stairs. God was really taking us for a ride.

We got played

I then revealed to Fabie that when we walked by the lady on the bench, I felt pulled to her.

"Maybe we're supposed to pray for her," she said.

"Okay, you're right," I responded.

We walked over to her, and Fabie asked if we could pray for her, and we were instantly denied.

"No, I don't do any of that prayer stuff," she said.

We're like, okay, ma'am, sorry to bother you. At this point, we looked up at the sky and said, "Okay, God... A little guidance, please?"

We decided God just didn't want us going to Atlantic Avenue. (Notice how I wrote we decided a lot. facepalm) So I placed a request for an Uber pool and put my phone in my pocket as it found me a ride, because I then immediately got the urge to sit down on a bench across the street.

"We need to follow where we're being led," I said as we started to cross the large road toward Nostrand Avenue. It was weird, because even though I felt like I needed to cross over to the other side, while on the crosswalk, in the middle of the street, I looked at Fabie and said, "I have a strong feeling we're going to have to walk back across this street again because our Uber is going to show up on the street we just left."

I kid you not!!

That was precisely what happened.

Y'all, I never looked at my phone, so I had no idea what direction the car was coming from. I literally placed the order for the Uber and stuffed my phone back in my pocket while it searched for the ride.

We crossed that wide street toward Nostrand, I took out my phone, and looked down at the app. The Uber pool was right in front of the Foot Locker diagonally across the street from where we just crossed.

As we were about to cross back over, my eyes caught on a homeless man sitting in front of the Dallas BBQ.

I told Fabie, and she said, "That's the connection. You were pulled to the homeless lady, but maybe it's him we're meant to pray for."

We figured God pulled me to the woman so that I could keep a lookout for someone who needed help and made me want to cross the street so that I could see him. I am usually always looking for ways to help the homeless, but God knew that I would get distracted by all the supernatural stuff that was going on, and He didn't want me to miss what He wanted us to do. Plus, both Fabie and I were pretty hell-bent on getting to the church.

A new friend

We headed over to the homeless man who was sitting with his belongings in front of the Dallas BBQ on top of a cardboard box. As we walked over, I noticed that he had a rosary around his neck. I thought:

At least we might not get played this time, LOL.

Needless to say, our Uber left us. It didn't matter though, as we now concluded that God wanted us to stay in the area.

As we walked over to him, Fabie asked, "Can we pray for you?"

He immediately said, "Of course," and pointed at his rosary.

(At this point, I was creeped out by my own accuracy or rather the accuracy of the Holy Spirit.) Fabie then prayed for him, but as she was praying, I was distracted. I looked at this man who was barefoot and had everything he owned on that cardboard box and was amazed at how he was still so open to God. The meek really shall inherit the Earth.

Anyway, Fabie finished her prayer, and I handed him some of the money I had received from the bodega. Fabie continued to talk with him and wished him well. Then honestly, out of nowhere, I heard myself say, _"What size shoe are you?"_

Who said that?!

I mean, it was my mouth, but it was clearly taken over by the Holy Spirit.

I honestly never even had the thought. The words just spilled out of my mouth. He told me he was a size twelve. Fabie offered him our leftovers, which he gladly accepted, and we let him know we would be back.

I looked over at Fabie and said, "I have to buy that man's shoes." She already knew. I wasn't the only one who heard the Holy Spirit hijack my voice.

Guess what shoe store was the only one open at that time on Sunday was? Ding-Ding-Ding: Foot Locker. We did have to cross the street... to exactly where our Uber was previously stationed.

Mind=Blown.

Only God can work things out like this.

We continued to cross those wide streets, and I kept asking Fabie and myself honestly, **"Who said that?"** It was like an out-of-body experience. Both Fabie and I, at this point, were in godly explorer mode.

Like what next, Jesus?

We looked at each other in disbelief and were just glad that we were going through it together.

Foot Locker

I told Fabie as we walked in that it needed to be a dark sneaker so he could be comfortable and it could stay clean. When we walked in, we were immediately greeted by a sales associate who asked if he could help us. I found the sneakers quickly. I mean, the perfect sneakers were sitting right there on the wall as we walked in. I picked it up and asked the guy for a size twelve.

Fabie and I just stared at each other in disbelief for a while.

We barely spoke and when we did talk, we were in pure wonder at what was happening to us.

Fabie and Franky not speaking is a miracle in itself... just saying.

While we were waiting for the sales associate, I felt the urge to get our new friend some clothes. Fabie and I were amazed at how God had us shopping for him as though he were our father or brother. I ended up getting two shirts. I wanted to get him an outfit, but it was summer and the only pants available were sweatpants and I thought they would be too hot for the weather.

The sales associate came back over and advised us that the shoes were at the counter, so we waited in the line behind a father and his son who were finishing up their purchase. While we were waiting, Fabie looked over across the street and said, "I need to go into that McDonald's."

Up until now, I felt like I was the main creepy person. Everything I said came to pass and it was secretly weirding me out. When Fabie said we needed to go into McDonald's, a "phew" came over my spirit. I silently thanked the Lord that He was dispensing some of this creepiness over to Fabie (although, in hindsight, the Holy Spirit was leading Fabie to pray the entire time).

I said, "God just wants to use us to help him feel human again." We concluded that I had to clothe him, and she had to feed him.

We got to the front of the line, and at this time, we were the last customers in the store. They had locked the doors and started to bring down the gates.

The cashier at the register apologized for taking so long. Honestly, we didn't notice the wait at all. We were so consumed by what God was doing that we didn't realize we had been waiting there for a bit while she helped the previous customers. We assured her that we were fine with the wait, and she started to ring us up. She began to make small talk with us, but both Fabie, and I were distracted. The burning question on our minds was: *"What next, Jesus?"*

I don't like talking about giving

Now I tried my best not to reveal what was going on and Fabie, knowing this about me, gets the gist, and we attempted to provide as little information as possible about what was going on.

I strongly believe in the passage in Matthew 6:3, where it reads: *"Do not let your left hand know what your right hand is doing."*

Being seen by my Father in heaven is enough for me. I also believe that this applies to what that person does with the money. I don't need to know. My God tells me to give, so I do it without any thought to what happens next. I figure if I think about it too much and try to ration my giving, I might miss someone who needed help because I was trying to control the situation.

Ultimately, my giving heart is not of my own doing but from God Himself. He gave me this heart so I can help others have a heart like His.

Honestly, that is part of the reason why I waited so long to share this story, but just like sharing this story, God had other plans then.

This was for her too

Now our small talk turned into: "These are nice shoes. Who are you buying these for?" We tried to work around that question with every ounce of our being without lying. She asked, "Is it a gift for your father? Brother? Uncle?" I did an internal facepalm, as we told her that we didn't know who it was for.

We told the truth. We didn't know our new friend. This seemed to intrigue her, and she proceeded to ask more questions. I then stopped and realized, "God, You want us to tell her, don't You? No one asks these questions. You hijacked her curiosity."

We then told her that we'd been on a journey with Jesus. Then the Holy Spirit hijacked my voice again, and I said He told us:

"Don't go to church...Be the Church."

Again, who said that? May I have my voice back, please, God?

We told her about what had been happening to us. We told her that no dollar vans were coming down Flatbush, which immediately garnered a look of disbelief.

We tell her how we happened upon our homeless friend and that these shoes were for him. She was immediately taken for a loop. She said: "I always want to help them, but I would rather buy food than give them money or clothes or anything because I'm afraid they will go buy drugs or something."

Fabie was up to bat.

This was something that Fabie also struggled with. She didn't want to be the cause of someone else's sin. However, in recent weeks, God changed her mindset and helped her see that He was ultimately the one in control and that other people's sin should not be her concern.

We were in the right place at the right time with the right combination of testimonies. I could bring the "God is in control" mindset, while Fabie could bring the "Girl, I understand where you're coming from."

Fabie was allowed to struggle through this precisely so she could have that conversation. That cashier had to know that Christians struggled too.

Again: Mind=Blown.

The cashier thought long and hard and said, "You know, I don't meet many people like you two." She marveled at the fact that she was now part of this epic story that was still unfolding. We said our goodbyes and wished her well and prayed her heart would open up to help others without needing to know everything about their situation. We let her know that giving money to the wrong person was far less a problem than missing out on the opportunity to help someone truly in need.

I'm not hungry

I paid for the sneakers and shirts, then we walked out of Foot Locker and headed back across the street to give our new friend his gifts. As we walked up to him, he sat up from a nap he had been taking and I said, "God put it on our hearts to buy you some new shoes today, and we have a few more items in there. I hope this helps you." He thanked me as I gave him some more money from my bodega change, and then Fabie said, "I'm heading to McDonald's, can I get you anything?"

He looked at us with this look of wonder in his eyes and said, "Oh, I'm not hungry! I just had steak and potatoes and so much more!"

Wait... What?

I don't know about you... but if I were homeless, I would have taken the food and saved it for later. But our new friend insisted that he was not hungry.

Y'all, when did he eat? When did this steak happen? In hindsight, that look of wonder was the Holy Spirit overtaking him. God fed him spiritually in a dream while we were in the store (facepalm).

Fabie and I were amazed. We wished him well and as we were walking away, I remembered that I never asked him his name.

"What is your name?" I asked.

"Tony," he said.

Wait a minute, Jesus. Do you mean to tell me this man has my husband's name? What was really happening here?

Fabie then went into her purse and gave him additional cash. **Y'all, Fabie gave him additional money without needing to know where it was going!**

McDonald's

We determined that God made our new friend Tony deny the food so we could go into that McDonald's for someone else. He didn't want us distracted. Fabie knew of another homeless man who sometimes hung out there. She felt that maybe this was why she was pulled there.

As we walked into McDonald's, I saw clothing on a table through the glass, and I said, "The person who owns those clothes needs help."

We assumed he was in the restroom. We waited for what seemed like an eternity but was in actuality probably fifteen minutes. Person after person walked by, but alas, they never sat down.

Finally, a woman walked over to the table with her food and was about to sit down when Fabie looked back at me and said, "I have to pray for her." She was clearly not homeless, but she was the owner of the clothing. We headed over, but I walked a little behind Fabie as I didn't want her to feel bombarded.

As we approached, the look on her face said, "Why are they heading this way?"

We walked up to her and promised her that we weren't crazy and that we believed God sent us here to pray for her. We promised that we weren't selling anything. We asked her if it was okay to pray for her, and she responded, "Well, I'll take this as a sign." Fabie started to pray for her, and I kid you not, this woman began to cry at the table in McDonald's in the middle of Fabie's prayer.

Her prayer was pretty simple. She said something along the lines of, "Lord, I don't know what she's going through right now, but we ask that You help her and to let her know that she is loved and that things will get better."

The moment that woman started to cry was confirmation that we were sent there for her. After Fabie's prayer ended, our new lady friend composed herself. She shared that she had been going through some hard times.

We talked for a little bit about how God had us on this journey all evening and she was part of it. I felt God push me to talk about dealing with MS and how sometimes God allows things to happen to teach us and the people around us a lesson.

Talking about my illness allowed her to feel a little more comfortable to share with two strangers that she had a family member who had been sick. She was the primary caregiver and was overwhelmed. I let her know that God is not surprised by our struggles and loves us through it. He is a good Father who wants us to learn and become better, and works all things out for our good. It hurts Him when we cry, but He knows the result is a stronger, better us.

Sometimes God will break your heart to save your soul.

Fabie also shared how my illness had taught her lessons about her own life. This helped our new friend to understand that sometimes someone else's trials are also for the people around them.

We continued to chat a little bit, and being from the melting pot of Brooklyn, we asked her the standard "Where is your family from?" question.

She said Haiti.

You guys, that was the kicker. We immediately started speaking as though we were old friends. We went in and out of two languages, talked about life being the children of Caribbean parents, funny quirks in Haitian/American families and so much more.

We laughed with her, made each other laugh, and had a great time. We believed that God also wanted us to make her smile. We also believed that being the main caregiver to her family member rarely gave her time for friends.

During our conversation, she revealed to us that she lived all the way out in Long Island and this was her last day traveling to Brooklyn to get her hair done, as she made this long trip without a car.

Her last day… Okay, Lord. Now You're just showing off.

She never really told us exactly what was wrong with her family member, but from how she spoke, we concluded that it might be cancer. As we talked, she told us things like this never happened to her. She was amazed at the entire encounter. Curious if God would show off again, we ask her what her family member's name was and get this… her first name was my maiden name. **Okay, God… okay.**

By this time, church service was clearly over. It was so late that we missed the two hours of after church socializing. Our friends had already made their way to Ippudo without me, and Tony was blowing up my phone. This was probably the only time I was happy that Ippudo had such a long wait time. It would take me at least forty-five minutes to get to the restaurant.

The overnight revival was about to start at Fabie's father's church, and I needed to be in Manhattan. We bid our new friend goodbye, and Fabie took her phone number. As we were walking out, we saw the homeless man Fabie was talking about. I handed Fabie the rest of the change I had from the bodega.

And just like that, I knew why the clerk at the bodega gave me my change like that.

We headed outside, and the sun had started to set. Fabie walked me to the train station as she no longer had a reason to leave the area. As we walked, we marveled at what just happened to us within the span of these few hours. We also honestly asked God if we were released from the area, because I mean, He got in the way for hours! We talked about how I still needed to get off at Atlantic to transfer, but agreed that maybe we just assumed that was what God meant.

I hugged her goodbye and was finally able to get on the train.

While on the train, I got a text from Tony that gave me new, faster directions, which would keep me from going through Atlantic Avenue. He did not yet know anything about what happened that night or that we thought God didn't want us on that street.

I guess God really was trying to prevent us from going to Atlantic Avenue after all.

I got off the train at 14th Street so I could transfer to the 6 train to get to Ipuddo. Tony then called me and said our table was ready and I had to get there quickly before they gave it away. The time on the train arrival clock read twelve minutes, and I just couldn't wait that long. I decided to walk. Now, my feet were hurting, I was exhausted, but I decided to walk anyway.

Walking down Broadway

I walked out of the train station and realized that I stepped onto the aftermath of the pride parade. As usual, after NYC parades, people were still hanging out on the streets, yelling, talking, etc. While I walked down the street, my spirit just became overwhelmed. I was overcome with love. I felt the love that God had for the people here. I was overwhelmed by the love the Most High God had for all people.

So, I prayed.

I prayed that everyone who was at this parade got home safe. I asked God to bless them and to keep them. I asked that He might show up in their lives like never before. I thanked Him for the adventure that He brought me on that day. Honestly, I thanked Him that even though my feet were blistering from walking in flats that were only meant for sitting, it was for a good reason.

It was the most I had walked in a very long time. I asked God to bless this city, to bless this country, and for His presence. A sense of peace settled in my heart as I pondered all the things that had happened.

Ippudo. Finally

I finally got to Ippudo. I was right on time, and we were seated immediately. I apologized to Tony and our friends for being late, to which they responded, "We were waiting for the table anyway." If you know Ippudo NY, their wait time is horrendous, but the food is just that good.

We sat down, ordered our food, and I got to tell them the entire story. Our friends were not Christians, but they were in wonder at the evening that I just had. I thanked God for this testimony and for using Fabie and me this way.

And thank You for dinner, Jesus. What a perfect way to end an amazing night!

Lessons and Blessings

Everyone involved in this story was blessed in some way.

Fabie: Fabie got to practice giving and got to minister to someone in a similar situation. She got to pray for people she didn't know and got to be on a spiritual shenanigan of her own. She also got to practice what God had been trying to teach her and put her prayer warrior skills to use in the middle of a lesson. I thank God that I have a friend like Fabie to be on holy shenanigans with. Best friends and PIPPS for **life!**

Foot Locker Representatives: The Foot Locker representatives learned there are people out there who truly seek to follow Jesus and that giving should not come with control.

Tony (new friend): Tony was blessed with some brand-new clothes and got to have some Haitian food. (After I got on the train, Fabie said she saw him eat the leftovers, proving that God snatched him up when he denied McDonald's.) Honestly, I believe that man has a very close relationship with God.

Woman in McDonald's: God showed her that He cares about her. He went out of His way to send two crazy women to pray for her and talk to her.

Tony (my husband): Tony learned never to underestimate the shenanigans that God will have me on. I honestly thank God for him because he is always down for when God has me in these situations and has even gotten into some holy shenanigans himself. I thank God that He gave me a husband who acknowledges His mysterious ways and who has a heart after His own.

Friends at Ippudo: They learned that God is working in tangible ways in the physical realm.

Me: I learned to trust that God speaks to and through me. I learned to follow where the Spirit leads me. I learned He will always lead me to where I am supposed to be, even if it feels like I took a detour through the woods.

There are so many more lessons I could mention, but for the sake of time, I'll leave it here.

The Ultimate Lesson:
WE wanted to go to church. **HE** wanted us to be the Church.

Obviously, all this happened pre-pandemic and pre-2020 craziness. Much like the past few years, God got in the way of our regularly scheduled church service to teach us that the Church is not a building.

In a sense, Fabie and I went on a mini-version of what the Church needs to do in the midst of this current storm.

Fabie and I didn't know what we got into on that seemingly normal Sunday, and I know a lot of us also feel the same about this pandemic and all of the other craziness going on. Much like when we asked to pray for the lady on the bench, we feel played. All of us had plans and now everything is canceled. Many people are pleading with God for: "A little guidance please?"

Ultimately, even though it feels like all these events are getting in the way, He shows us that these roadblocks are actually openings to get us to where we actually need to be.

If we're being honest.... these past couple of years feels like one giant roadblock.

I believe this is where we need to be. God is waking up His Church. This is when His people are needed the most. Bride of Christ, we need to stand up!

As we moved through the streets of Flatbush, we were privileged to be the physical representation of God. People who saw us saw God's love. We were confused the entire time, but our obedience was all He needed to touch people's lives through us.

As believers, we are privileged to have God to walk us through the troubles of this world. But for others, we are the only Bible that some people will ever read.

If we had gone to church that day, all those people would not have been blessed.

In the end, we learned:

Going to church fills us up.
Being the Church fills us and others.

How wonderful it would be if we all moved in obedience to God. All the time!

God is doing a new thing!

I no longer believe in coincidences. I don't believe it's a coincidence that Fabie had to be at a revival that night. I believe God is changing His Church from a place of complacency and reviving us with a spirit of action.

We have been commissioned to lead this change, and we were created for such a time as this. I strongly believe we are approaching a time where we will move like the first Christians: in power and in God's glory.

The physical building will have its purpose, but God is about to move mightily and He is raising up His children to take their rightful places as kings and queens. We will heal the sick, help the poor, seek the brokenhearted, and cast out demons for His name's sake.

Ultimately, If God wants to use us, He will use us, even when we're fighting to go in the opposite direction that He needs us to. If we depend on His guidance each step of the way, He will lead us into wonders and testimonies that we **never knew we needed.**

Arise! Bride of Christ! Let's Move like He's our God!

The Final Say

God is awesome

"For the Lord Most High is Awesome, the great King over all the earth"~ Psalm 47:2,NIV

S ometimes we forget to pray. Sometimes things will either be going so well or so badly that we go right back to depending on God for only the big things. It's happened to me and I still struggle at times. However, whenever we recognize that we are overwhelmed and burdened by life's troubles, or if we recognize that our Bible is collecting dust, it is God's Holy Spirit trying to get our attention. Trials are an invitation to pray, and so are good times.

If we acknowledge that we are the ones who moved, and repent, God is gracious enough to accept us back with open arms. There's a saying that says God will not give you more than you can bear. That saying is not found anywhere in the Bible. God gives people more than they can bear all the time. We can take solace that He always has a point in allowing the troubles in our lives. He says His yoke is light and He wants to trade our yoke for His because He is the only one strong enough to carry it. It's our dependence that He's after.

We just have to admit that we need help. The cross bore all those burdens, and His resurrection threw them into the fire with His victory. His check cleared.

The awesome thing about our God is that He made us for Himself and knows every intricate detail of our lives. He made us so He must know us. Even when we break His heart, He still welcomes us back and pursues us with open arms.

Unlike people who get annoyed at someone always coming to them for help (let's be honest saints, you too), He actually wants us to bother Him. He wants us to tell Him all our cares because He loves us. He wants to protect us from the schemes of the enemy and He wants us to dwell in eternity with Him.

He loved us so much that He sent His only Son, Jesus, to die the most gruesome death for us so we might become His sons and daughters, even when we didn't deserve it.

> *But God demonstrates his one love for us in this: While we were yet sinners, Christ died for us. (Rom. 5:8)*

His payment is permanent. Don't let the roach convince you otherwise.

Early in my walk, a priest held a mass that I will never forget. He said, "How many of you, even though you love your dog, would turn into a dog to save it?" No one raised their hands. Then he said, "That's what Jesus did for us." That sermon stuck with me because I love my dogs, but never would I turn into a dog to save them. Then again, my last name isn't Christ. I'm sinful and imperfect and Jesus is holy and awesome!

How great is our God that we get to call Him friend, Father, God and Lord. Thank you, Lord, that we are fighting from a place of victory and all our hope is in Your precious and holy name. Thank You, Jesus, for Your sacrifice. Thank You that Your spirit dwells within me and those You care for. I pray for every single one of these readers. I pray for a hedge of protection over them as well as a newfound love for Your ways and for depending on You in all of life's circumstances. I thank You that petty prayers are where You work Your best and You want us to come to You with all our burdens, and you are strong enough to carry them. Thank You, Lord, that You care for us, for creating us, and for knowing us in every single way.

Thank You, Lord, that You want a relationship with us and You have chosen us for such a time as this. In Jesus' name I pray. Amen.

Now Go Out and Be **P**etty.

CPSIA information can be obtained
at www.ICGtesting.com
Printed in the USA
LVHW011653030322
712534LV00008B/178